LUTHER'S WORKS

American Edition

VOLUME 42

*Published by Concordia Publishing House
and Fortress Press in 55 volumes.
General Editors are Jaroslav Pelikan (for vols. 1-30)
and Helmut T. Lehmann (for vols. 31-55)*

LUTHER'S WORKS

VOLUME 42

Devotional Writings

I

EDITED BY

MARTIN O. DIETRICH

GENERAL EDITOR

HELMUT T. LEHMANN

FORTRESS PRESS / PHILADELPHIA

GENERAL EDITORS'
PREFACE

The first editions of Luther's collected works appeared in the sixteenth century, and so did the first efforts to make him "speak English." In America serious attempts in these directions were made for the first time in the nineteenth century. The Saint Louis edition of Luther was the first endeavor on American soil to publish a collected edition of his works, and the Henkel Press in Newmarket, Virginia, was the first to publish some of Luther's writings in an English translation. During the first decade of the twentieth century, J. N. Lenker produced translations of Luther's sermons and commentaries in thirteen volumes. A few years later the first of the six volumes in the Philadelphia (or Holman) edition of the *Works of Martin Luther* appeared. But a growing recognition of the need for more of Luther's works in English has resulted in this American edition of Luther's works.

The edition is intended primarily for the reader whose knowledge of late medieval Latin and sixteenth-century German is too small to permit him to work with Luther in the original languages. Those who can will continue to read Luther in his original words as these have been assembled in the monumental Weimar edition (*D. Martin Luthers Werke*. Kritische Gesamtausgabe, Weimar, 1883-   ). Its texts and helps have formed a basis for this edition, though in certain places we have felt constrained to depart from its readings and findings. We have tried throughout to translate Luther as he thought translating should be done. That is, we have striven for faithfulness on the basis of the best lexicographical materials available. But where literal accuracy and clarity have conflicted, it is clarity that we have preferred, so that sometimes paraphrase seemed more faithful than literal fidelity. We have proceeded in a similar way in the matter of Bible versions, translating Luther's translation. Where this could be done by the use of an existing English version—King James, Douay, or Revised Standard—we have

v

done so. Where it could not, we have supplied our own. To indicate this in each specific instance would have been pedantic; to adopt a uniform procedure would have been artificial—especially in view of Luther's own inconsistency in this regard. In each volume the translator will be responsible primarily for matters of text and language, while the responsibility of the editor will extend principally to the historical and theological matters reflected in the introductions and notes.

Although the edition as planned will include fifty-five volumes, Luther's writings are not being translated in their entirety. Nor should they be. As he was the first to insist, much of what he wrote and said was not that important. Thus the edition is a selection of works that have proved their importance for the faith, life, and history of the Christian church. The first thirty volumes contain Luther's expositions of various biblical books, while the remaining volumes include what are usually called his "Reformation writings" and other occasional pieces. The final volume of the set will be an index volume; in addition to an index of quotations, proper names, and topics, and a list of corrections and changes, it will contain a glossary of many of the technical terms that recur in Luther's works and that cannot be defined each time they appear. Obviously Luther cannot be forced into any neat set of rubrics. He can provide his reader with bits of autobiography or with political observations as he expounds a psalm, and he can speak tenderly about the meaning of the faith in the midst of polemics against his opponents. It is the hope of publishers, editors, and translators that through this edition the message of Luther's faith will speak more clearly to the modern church.

J. P.
H. T. L.

CONTENTS

BG — *Luthers Werke für das christliche Haus,* edited by Georg Buchwald (Braunschweig, 1889-1892).

CIC — *Corpus Iuris Canonici,* edited by E. Friedberg (Graz, 1955).

C.R. — *Corpus Reformatorum,* edited by C. G. Bretschneider and H. E. Bindseil (Halle/Saale, 1834-1860).

LW — American Edition of *Luther's Works* (Philadelphia and St. Louis, 1955-   ).

MA³ — *Martin Luther.* Ausgewählte Werke, 3rd edition (München, 1948-   ).

PE — *Works of Martin Luther.* Philadelphia Edition (Philadelphia, 1915-1943).

St. L. — D. *Martin Luthers sämmtliche Schriften,* edited by Johann Georg Walch. Edited and published in modern German, 23 vols. in 25 (2nd ed.; St. Louis, 1880-1910).

WA — D. *Martin Luthers Werke.* Kritische Gesamtausgabe (Weimar, 1883-   ).

WA, Br — D. *Martin Luthers Werke.* Briefwechsel (Weimar, 1930-   ).

WA, DB — D. *Martin Luthers Werke.* Deutsche Bibel (Weimar, 1906-1961).

WA, TR — D. *Martin Luthers Werke.* Tischreden (Weimar, 1912-1921).

INTRODUCTION TO
Devotional Writings

On October 19, 1512, less than a month before his twenty-ninth birthday, Martin Luther received the degree of doctor of theology. Within that very week he was admitted to the theological faculty of the University of Wittenberg as professor of Bible and began his teaching career by lecturing on the Book of Genesis. These three events coalesce to rank in significance with the storm at Stotternheim[1] and the "tower experience," [2] for they shaped and molded the rest of his life and work. Again and again Luther spoke of what his doctoral oath and office meant to him. Typical of his comments on the subject is the statement in his 1532 treatise *Infiltrating and Clandestine Preachers*, "I have often said and still say, I would not exchange my doctor's degree for all the world's gold. For I would surely in the long run lose courage and fall into despair if, as these infiltrators, I had undertaken these great and serious matters without call or commission. But God and the whole world bears me testimony that I entered this work publicly and by virtue of my office as teacher and preacher, and have carried it on hitherto by the grace and help of God." [3] This oath and office played their part in releasing Luther from the shackles of his personal quest for salvation by imposing upon him what was not just an academic, but an essentially pastoral vocation.

Luther's entire career as a professor and reformer involved the exercise of his pastoral vocation in three distinct areas of activity.

---

[1] On July 2, 1505, Luther was caught in a thunderstorm near the village of Stotternheim. Knocked to the ground and thoroughly terrified, Luther cried out, "St. Anne, help me. I will become a monk." Fifteen days later, on July 17, he presented himself at the Augustinian cloister at Erfurt.

[2] The term "tower experience" refers to Luther's arrival at the conclusion some time between 1508 and 1518 that "if we, as righteous men, ought to live from faith and if the righteousness of God should contribute to the salvation of all who believe, then salvation won't be our merit but God's mercy." *LW* 54, 193-194.

[3] *LW* 40, 387-388.

First, he exercised this vocation in the classroom, primarily with students of theology. Nonetheless, for Luther theology was not a detached academic pursuit circumscribed by the walls, procedures, customs, and language of the university, but a matter of life and death. He took God seriously. Nothing is more important in man's life than his relationship to God. The chief function of theology (and of the theologian), then, is not to speculate about God[4] or even to systematize man's knowledge of God. Rather its function is to lead men to and strengthen them in faith. For Luther faith meant specifically trust in God through Jesus Christ. Inevitably Luther's classroom extended far beyond the university and the circle of educated students to whom he lectured there.

Second, Luther exercised his pastoral vocation in the area of preaching. In May, 1512, he was appointed subprior of the Augustinian monastery at Wittenberg. This appointment involved preaching in the cloister and in the town church, whose pastor was ailing. Even after a successor to the pastor was appointed in 1522 Luther was a frequent and often steady occupant of the town church pulpit. In addition, Luther preached on occasion at the castle church and elsewhere. It has been estimated that between 1522 and 1546 he preached at least seventy times a year. In later years he recalled that in the year 1517 he preached as much as four times a day.[5]

The third area in which Luther exercised his pastoral vocation was that of personal counsel and assistance. One evening his sleep was interrupted by a messenger from the widow of the recently deceased pastor of a nearby village. The burden of her urgent request was that Dr. Luther should find a husband for her. With no little irritation Luther dismissed the messenger with the reply that the widow should find a new husband on her own. After the messenger had left Luther laughed and said to a house guest that he would do what he could for the widow.[6]

Quite apart from its humor, this item of Table Talk illustrates that despite his heavy workload, Luther was in constant touch with life on the most mundane as well as the most ethereal levels. Because of his prominence he was frequently called upon by those of high

---

[4] "True theology is practical, and its foundation is Christ, whose death is appropriated to us through faith. . . . Accordingly speculative theology belongs to the devil in hell." LW 54, 22.
[5] On Luther's career as a preacher, see LW 51, xi-xxi.
[6] LW 54, 155.

and low estate for advice, help, and even arbitration. Indeed, just the day before he died Luther had successfully completed the arbitration of a dispute between the counts of Mansfeld.

Much of this counsel, advice, and opinion was given in his books, letters, and other writings, many of which were occasioned by specific pastoral situations. The writings presented in the two volumes of the American Edition of *Luther's Works* designated "Devotional Writings" [7] reflect the three areas in which Luther exercised his pastoral vocation. These works do not demonstrate external procedures and techniques by which Luther applied his theology. Rather, they demonstrate the faith out of which the theology issued. [8]

The first volume of "Devotional Writings" illustrates Luther's exercise of his pastoral vocation during the crucial years of 1519 to 1521. In 1519 the Spaniard Hapsburg Charles V was elected emperor of the Holy Roman Empire. In that same year John Eck, the sharp Dominican theologian, maneuvered Luther into a virtual admission of heresy at their debate in Leipzig, and the German nationalist leaders Ulrich von Hutten and Francis von Sickingen embraced Luther's cause as their own, thus making Luther a German hero. In 1520 Luther fired some of his most devastating literary artillery against Rome, [9] and in addition burned the papal bull *Exsurge, Domine* at the Elster Gate of Wittenberg. And chief of the great and tumultuous events of 1521 was Luther's appearance before the Diet of Worms and his subsequent disappearance from the public scene to the seclusion of the Wartburg Castle.

The contents of the second volume range over the years 1522 to 1545, the year before Luther's death. These were the years during which the Reformation underwent the transition from a movement within the Roman church to a distinct and separate expression of the Christian faith. It was also during these years that the diversity of the Reformation asserted itself and the antecedents of Protestant denominations began to emerge. Luther, although still a towering figure, was no longer *the* Reformer, but one of several.

M.O.D.

---

[7] On the term "devotional writings," see *LW* 43, xi.
[8] On the interrelation between Luther's "spiritual counsel" and his theology, see Theodore G. Tappert (ed.), *Luther: Letters of Spiritual Counsel* ("Library of Christian Classics," Vol. XVIII [Philadelphia: Westminster Press, 1955]), pp. 14-15.
[9] See in this volume, pp. xiii-xiv.

INTRODUCTION TO VOLUME 42

Until he posted his theses[1] in 1517, Martin Luther was a relatively obscure Augustinian monk, preacher, and professor at the not particularly prestigious University of Wittenberg. As the content of these theses became known, Luther was catapulted into fame among sympathizers and infamy among opponents. By calling into question not only the administration, but the very validity of the Roman church's system of indulgences, the Reformer became the midwife of the widespread yet varied movement which had been gestating for more than two centuries.[2] By the end of 1521 he was the most controversial figure on the European continent and the hero of the German nation. During these four years he moved steadily and rapidly away from medieval Catholicism toward an evangelical Christianity. What began as a rather hesitant, almost reluctant, questioning of a single aspect of the church's teaching and practice soon extended to the whole political, social, ethical, and theological structure of Western civilization.

It was during these four tumultuous years between the posting of the theses and the sojourn at the Wartburg Castle that the works constituting this volume of devotional writings were composed, published, and widely read. During these years of crisis, upheaval, and maneuvering Luther wrote some of his most explosive and shattering treatises. In the year 1520 alone he produced, among other writings, three major works. In his *Treatise on Good Works*[3] he demolished the entire medieval concept of works-righteousness. *To the Christian Nobility of the German Nation*[4] was a ringing indictment of ecclesiastical and social error and abuse along with specific proposals for reform. (Significantly, many of these proposals were ultimately accepted by the Second Vatican Council.) In *The Baby-*

---

[1] Cf. the *Ninety-five Theses. LW* 31, 17-33.
[2] On the types of reform movements, see B. A. Gerrish (ed.), *Reformers in Profile* (Philadelphia: Fortress Press, 1967), pp. 2-9.
[3] *LW* 44, 15-114.
[4] *LW* 44, 115-217.

lonian Captivity of the Church[5] Luther assailed the sacramental system of the Roman church, which covered every aspect of human life. These and other writings of this period are works forged on the hot iron of controversy.

The seven devotional writings presented here, however, stand in such marked contrast to the other writings of this period that the reader who is only slightly familiar with Luther cannot fail to note the difference. This contrast can be illustrated in four distinct particulars.

First, the reader will note the almost total absence of polemic. To be sure, Luther is critical; he does cite abuses and errors. But these passages are amazingly mild, even subdued, in tone. There is no sensationalism about them.

Second, there is about these writings an air of detachment from the specific historical events and circumstances in which Luther was enveloped. His very life was literally at stake. Yet he neither speaks nor alludes to these circumstances. Perhaps it is precisely this very absence of personal and contextual references which adds strength and vitality to what he has to say. The truth he espouses and affirms transcends even the struggles in which he is engaged, although his messages clearly reflect his own inner experience. Thus the preacher-pastor subordinates himself and his struggles to the message with which he is entrusted and to which he is committed.

Third, there is a disciplined brevity in these writings which is by no means characteristic of Luther.[6] He sticks very closely to the theme and issue at hand, drawing almost solely on the Bible rather than on the fathers or other sources for specific and relevant illustration and amplification of the point he wants to make.

Fourth, these writings exhibit a distinct restraint on the part of the Reformer. Although intellectually and religiously far advanced beyond those to whom he addresses himself, Luther begins where they are. He still employs the forms, terminology, and imagery which shaped the piety and thus the whole religious outlook of his era, but he uses them to communicate the gospel. He does so without compromising the gospel.

A Meditation on Christ's Passion (1519) speaks to Christians long accustomed to a Good Friday vigil at the cross. To keep this

---

[5] *LW* 36, 3-126.
[6] On Luther's preaching style, see *LW* 51, xvi-xvii.

vigil and to commemorate the passion was the accepted thing to do. But many who did it out of piety did it for the wrong reasons and therefore with no genuine spiritual benefit. Luther does not hesitate to say so. He resolves the situation, however, not by assailing or discarding a long-standing practice, but by emphasizing the proper contemplation of Christ's suffering on the cross and what it can accomplish for the Christian.

An Exposition of the Lord's Prayer for Simple Laymen (1519) is really more than what the title implies. In expositing the universal prayer of Christians Luther does far more than dissect and analyze the parts of a whole. At bottom he is dealing with the whole matter of prayer, the great hallmark of Christian piety, but, at the same time, the great obstacle of the Christian's life.

Similarly, in *On Rogationtide Prayer and Procession* (1519) Luther instructs his hearers and readers how to pray. Prayer is not a question of form or posture or words, but of faith, and faith lies at the heart of man's response to the gospel of Christ. Nor is Luther's treatment of prayer the kind of thing one expects of a pastor simply as a matter of course. If anything stands out in this sermon (indeed, in all of the writings of this volume), it is the impression of a pastor sharing with a congregation that which he himself has experienced, without imposing his person or his experience as such upon his people.

A Sermon on Preparing to Die (1519) deals with an issue to which Luther was no stranger. The heart of his message is salvation through faith in Christ. The dread of medieval man was death. For Luther the death of Christ, through man's trusting faith in him, destroys the terror that dying holds for Christian believers.

The writing of the *Fourteen Consolations* (1520) must have confronted Luther with some uneasiness, not to mention difficulty. Written for Elector Frederick the Wise during that prince's serious illness in 1519, Luther could easily have exploited the circumstances to his own advantage. Nonetheless, except for occasional and unmistakable references to the Elector, he could have been writing for his barber.[7] Luther provided the kind of guidance and food for thought which the seriously ill can dwell upon with profit, the kind

---

[7] Luther did in fact write a little book for his barber. See *A Simple Way to Pray* (1535). LW 43, 187-211.

of things which illness compels a man—even a powerful, medieval prince—to think about.

The Lord's Supper has always posed a great variety of historical and doctrinal problems for Christians. In addition to essentially academic questions, there has always been the religious problem: the individual Christian's understanding of and attitude toward the sacrament. In Luther's day the Lord's Supper, embodied in the mass and its theology of sacrifice and works-righteousness, was abused and distorted not only by church doctrine, but by popular beliefs and practices as well. Less than a week before his departure for Worms to face the authorities of church and empire, Luther calmly preached his *Sermon on the Worthy Reception of the Sacrament* (1521).

The last piece in this volume, *Comfort When Facing Grave Temptations* (1521), also deals with a facet of life with which Luther was personally quite familiar. In addition to having faith in Christ, the Christian, since he belongs to the communion of saints (and thus to Christ himself), has the church invisible to strengthen and comfort him in his distress.

M. O. D.

LUTHER'S WORKS

VOLUME 42

A MEDITATION ON CHRIST'S PASSION

1519

Translated by Martin H. Bertram

INTRODUCTION

On Invocavit Sunday, March 13, 1519, Luther wrote his friend George Spalatin, "I am planning a treatise dealing with the meditation of Christ's passion. I do not know, however, whether I shall have enough leisure to write it out. Yet I shall try hard." [1] In the same letter he cites the reasons for this lack of leisure: activities directed toward the renewal of the university curriculum, his work on the Lord's Prayer,[2] a commentary on Galatians, and particularly pressing and irksome, his intense study of canon law in preparation for the upcoming Leipzig Debate with John Eck, July 4 to 14. Nevertheless, it was a mere three weeks later, on April 5, that Luther was able to send a printed copy of his work on the passion to Spalatin.[3]

By 1524, a total of twenty-four editions had been printed in Wittenberg, Basel, Augsburg, Zurich, Erfurt, Munich, Nürnberg, and Strassburg. The number of editions testifies to the widespread response aroused by this writing. A Latin edition, whose translator is unknown, appeared at Wittenberg in 1521. As the sermon for Good Friday, this treatise was included in the *Church Postil* of 1525, which Luther termed his "very best book." [4]

The quick and widespread acceptance of this tract attests to the inner needs of the common people. Writings such as this, with their pastoral emphasis, attracted even more readers than those concerned with protest. While no single, specific cause can be cited which impelled a polemically busy Luther to write such a treatise, it can be assumed that his contact with the people in the parish forced him to take note of the areas in which the search for peace and salvation was most desperate. Although deep-rooted tradition provided the form in which they were embodied, the thoughts expressed by Luther were the early fruit of his evolving theology.

---

[1] *LW* 48, 114. Such meditations on the sufferings of Christ were a popular form of Lenten devotion during the Middle Ages. *MA*³ 1, 520.
[2] See in this volume, *An Exposition of the Lord's Prayer for Simple Laymen*, pp. 15-81.
[3] *WA*, Br 1, 367.
[4] *WA* 10ᴵ, 1-2; 17ᴵᴵ, 21-22.

In the first three numbered paragraphs Luther discusses the false attitudes toward Christ's suffering which are based on blaming the Jews, on seeking a superficial benefit from the sufferings, and on a sentimental commiseration with Christ. Paragraphs four to eleven deal with the proper contemplation of the sufferings of Christ, stressing the need of seeing one's own sin as the cause of Christ's suffering, and how such knowledge should affect our faith and life. Moving from the cross to the comfort and assurance of Easter, Luther then arrives at the necessity of placing all our sin on Christ and emulating in our lives the qualities that Christ evidenced as he suffered for us.

Most of the twenty-four editions have title woodcuts showing the crucified Christ, with Mary and John standing at the foot of the cross. Others have woodcuts showing either Christ with an unidentified man kneeling before him, Christ sitting on a rock surrounded by instruments of torture, Christ at prayer in Gethsemane, or Christ and the torture instruments, with Christ holding a chalice in his left hand.

The translation is based on the German text, *Ein Sermon von der Betrachtung des heiligen Leidens Christi,* in WA 2, (130) 136-142. A copy of this version is extant in the State Library in Munich and bears a dedication in Luther's handwriting: "P Magistro Venceslao. . . ." [5]

---

[5] Wenceslas Link, a close friend of Luther, was a preacher at Nürnberg. This text is accepted as the original, for it is unlikely that Luther would have dedicated any but the first print to one of his friends. Cf. *LW* 48, 169-170.

A MEDITATION ON
CHRIST'S PASSION

1. Some people meditate on Christ's passion by venting their anger on the Jews.[1] This singing and ranting about wretched Judas[2] satisfies them, for they are in the habit of complaining about other people, of condemning and reproaching their adversaries. That might well be a meditation on the wickedness of Judas and the Jews, but not on the sufferings of Christ.

2. Some point to the manifold benefits and fruits that grow from contemplating Christ's passion. There is a saying ascribed to Albertus[3] about this, that it is more beneficial to ponder Christ's passion just once than to fast a whole year or to pray a psalm daily, etc. These people follow this saying blindly and therefore do not reap the fruit of Christ's passion, for in so doing they are seeking their own advantage. They carry pictures and booklets, letters and crosses on their person. Some who travel afar do this in the belief that they thus protect themselves against water and sword, fire, and all sorts of perils.[4] Christ's suffering is thus used to effect in them a lack of suffering contrary to his being and nature.

3. Some feel pity for Christ, lamenting and bewailing his innocence. They are like the women who followed Christ from Jeru-

---

[1] Luther's attitude toward the Jews finds frequent expression in his works. At the beginning of his career his position was one of benevolent hope of converting them to Christianity. This is reflected in this treatise, as well as in his *That Christ Was Born a Jew*, 1523 (*LW* 45, 195-229). Over the years his position changed, due largely to the adamant refusal of the Jews to accept his invitation to acknowledge Christ. This is evidenced in his treatise of 1547, *On the Jews and Their Lies*. WA 53, (412) 417-552.

[2] Luther alludes to a medieval German hymn, *O du armer Judas, was hast du getan* ("Ah, Thou Wretched Judas, What Is It You Have Done?"). MA[3] 1, 520.

[3] Albert Magnus (1193-1280) was a scholastic theologian, often called *"Doctor universalis,"* and a teacher of Thomas Aquinas.

[4] Luther here directs his criticism at those who carry holy pictures, prayer books (cf. *LW* 43, 5-7), rosaries, etc., as amulets to ward off harm and danger, as well as those who undertake pilgrimages.

salem and were chided and told by Christ that it would be better to weep for themselves and their children [Luke 23:27-28]. They are the kind of people who go far afield in their meditation on the passion, making much of Christ's farewell from Bethany[5] and of the Virgin Mary's anguish,[6] but never progressing beyond that, which is why so many hours are devoted to the contemplation of Christ's passion. Only God knows whether that is invented for the purpose of sleeping or of waking.[7]

Also to this group belong those who have learned what rich fruits the holy mass offers. In their simplemindedness they think it enough simply to hear mass. In support of this several teachers are cited to us who hold that the mass is *opere operati, non opere operantis*,[8] that it is effective in itself without our merit and worthiness, and that this is all that is needed. Yet the mass was not instituted for its own worthiness, but to make us worthy and to remind us of the passion of Christ. Where that is not done, we make of the mass a physical and unfruitful act, though even this is of some good. Of what help is it to you that God is God, if he is not God to you?[9] Of what benefit is it to you that food and drink are good and wholesome in themselves if they are not healthful for you? And it is to be feared that many masses will not improve matters as long as we do not seek the right fruit in them.

4. They contemplate Christ's passion aright who view it with a terror-stricken heart and a despairing conscience. This terror must be felt as you witness the stern wrath and the unchanging earnestness with which God looks upon sin and sinners, so much so that he was unwilling to release sinners even for his only and dearest Son

---

[5] John 12:1-8. The veneration of Martha was widespread in medieval Germany. See Stephen Beissel, *Geschichte der Verehrung Marthas in Deutschland während des Mittelalters* (Freiburg, 1909).
[6] John 19:25-27.
[7] It was not unusual for such contemplations to last four or five hours. Often they were much longer, and the pious frequently fell asleep. On these devotional exercises, see Florenz Landmann, *Das Predigtwesen in Westfalen in der letzten Zeit des Mittelalters* (Münster, 1900), p. 75.
[8] I.e., the mechanical performance of the mass makes it valid and effective, not the inward intent or disposition of the one who celebrates the mass.
[9] Ever more pronounced from this point on is Luther's emphasis on the *pro me, pro nobis* ("for me, for us"), reflecting the personal aspect of faith which Luther himself experienced and now expressed in all his writings.

without his payment of the severest penalty for them. Thus he says in Isaiah 53 [:8], "I have chastised him for the transgressions of my people." If the dearest child is punished thus, what will be the fate of sinners?[10] It must be an inexpressible and unbearable earnestness that forces such a great and infinite person to suffer and die to appease it. And if you seriously consider that it is God's very own Son, the eternal wisdom of the Father, who suffers, you will be terrified indeed. The more you think about it, the more intensely will you be frightened.

5. You must get this thought through your head and not doubt that you are the one who is torturing Christ thus, for your sins have surely wrought this. In Acts 2 [:36-37] St. Peter frightened the Jews like a peal of thunder when he said to all of them, "You crucified him." Consequently three thousand alarmed and terrified Jews asked the apostles on that one day, "O dear brethren, what shall we do now?" Therefore, when you see the nails piercing Christ's hands, you can be certain that it is your work. When you behold his crown of thorns, you may rest assured that these are your evil thoughts, etc.

6. For every nail that pierces Christ, more than one hundred thousand should in justice pierce you, yes, they should prick you forever and ever more painfully! When Christ is tortured by nails penetrating his hands and feet, you should eternally suffer the pain they inflict and the pain of even more cruel nails, which will in truth be the lot of those who do not avail themselves of Christ's passion. This earnest mirror,[11] Christ, will not lie or trifle, and whatever it points out will come to pass in full measure.

7. St. Bernard[12] was so terrified by this that he declared, "I regarded myself secure; I was not aware of the eternal sentence that had been passed on me in heaven until I saw that God's only Son had compassion upon me and offered to bear this sentence for me. Alas, if the situation is that serious, I should not make light of it or feel secure." We read that Christ commanded the women not to weep for him but for themselves and their children [Luke 23:28].

---

[10] Cf. Luke 23:31.

[11] I.e., the one in and through whom we see our sin in its starkness.

[12] St. Bernard of Clairvaux (1090-1153), Cistercian monk, mystic, and founder of the abbey of Clairvaux, was held in high regard and frequently quoted by Luther.

And he adds the reason for this, saying, "For if they do this to the green wood, what will happen when it is dry?" [Luke 23:31] He says as it were: From my martyrdom you can learn what it is that you really deserve and what your fate should be. Here the saying applies that the small dog is whipped to frighten the big dog. Thus the prophet[13] said that all the generations on earth will bewail themselves over him; he does not say that they will bewail him, but that they will bewail themselves because of him. In like manner the people of whom we heard in Acts 2 [:36-37] were so frightened that they said to the apostles, "O brethren, what shall we do?" This is also the song of the church: "I will ponder this diligently and, as a result, my soul will languish within me." [14]

8. We must give ourselves wholly to this matter, for the main benefit of Christ's passion is that man sees into his own true self and that he be terrified and crushed by this. Unless we seek that knowledge, we do not derive much benefit from Christ's passion. The real and true work of Christ's passion is to make man conformable to Christ, so that man's conscience is tormented by his sins in like measure as Christ was pitiably tormented in body and soul by our sins. This does not call for many words but for profound reflection and a great awe of sins. Take this as an illustration: a criminal is sentenced to death for the murder of the child of a prince or a king. In the meantime you go your carefree way, singing and playing, until you are cruelly arrested and convicted of having inspired the murderer. Now the whole world closes in upon you, especially since your conscience also deserts you. You should be terrified even more by the meditation on Christ's passion. For the evildoers, the Jews, whom God has judged and driven out, were only the servants of your sin; you are actually the one who, as we said, by his sin killed and crucified God's Son.

9. He who is so hardhearted and callous as not to be terrified by Christ's passion and led to a knowledge of self, has reason to fear. For it is inevitable, whether in this life or in hell, that you will

---

13 Cf. Jer. 4:31.

14 This hymn cannot be named with certainty, though it may well have been Bernard of Clairvaux's *Salve Caput cruentatem*, later paraphrased freely by Paul Gerhard in his "O Sacred Head Now Wounded."

have to become conformable to Christ's image and suffering.[15] At the very least, you will sink into this terror in the hour of death and in purgatory[16] and will tremble and quake and feel all that Christ suffered on the cross. Since it is horrible to lie waiting on your deathbed, you should pray God to soften your heart and let you now ponder Christ's passion with profit to you. Unless God inspires our heart, it is impossible for us of ourselves to meditate thoroughly on Christ's passion. No meditation or any other doctrine is granted to you that you might be boldly inspired by your own will to accomplish this. You must first seek God's grace and ask that it be accomplished by his grace and not by your own power. That is why the people we referred to above fail to view Christ's passion aright. They do not seek God's help for this, but look to their own ability to devise their own means of accomplishing this. They deal with the matter in a completely human but also unfruitful way.

10. We say without hesitation that he who contemplates God's sufferings for a day, an hour, yes, only a quarter of an hour, does better than to fast a whole year, pray a psalm daily, yes, better than to hear a hundred masses. This meditation changes man's being and, almost like baptism, gives him a new birth. Here the passion of Christ performs its natural and noble work, strangling the old Adam and banishing all joy, delight, and confidence which man could derive from other creatures, even as Christ was forsaken by all, even by God.

11. Since this [strangling of the old Adam] does not rest with us, it happens that we occasionally pray for it, and yet do not attain it at once. Nevertheless we should neither despair nor desist. At times this happens because we do not pray for it as God conceives of it and wishes it, for it must be left free and unfettered. Then man becomes sad in his conscience and grumbles to himself about the evil in his life. It may well be that he does not know that Christ's passion, to which he gives no thought, is effecting this in him, even as the others who do think of Christ's passion still do not gain this knowledge of self through it. For these the passion of Christ is hidden and genuine, while for those it is only unreal and mislead-

---

[15] Cf. I Cor. 15:49.
[16] At this point in his career Luther did not question the doctrine of purgatory.

ing. In that way God often reverses matters, so that those who do not meditate on Christ's passion do meditate on it, and those who do not hear mass do hear it, and those who hear it do not hear it.

12. Until now we have sojourned in Passion Week and rightly celebrated Good Friday.[17] Now we come to the resurrection of Christ, to the day of Easter. After man has thus become aware of his sin and is terrified in his heart, he must watch that sin does not remain in his conscience, for this would lead to sheer despair. Just as [our knowledge of] sin flowed from Christ and was acknowledged by us, so we must pour this sin back on him and free our conscience of it. Therefore beware, lest you do as those perverse people who torture their hearts with their sins and strive to do the impossible, namely, get rid of their sins by running from one good work or penance to another, or by working their way out of this by means of indulgences. Unfortunately such false confidence in penance and pilgrimages is widespread.[18]

13. You cast your sins from yourself and onto Christ when you firmly believe that his wounds and sufferings are your sins, to be borne and paid for by him, as we read in Isaiah 53 [:6], "The Lord has laid on him the iniquity of us all." St. Peter says, "in his body has he borne our sins on the wood of the cross" [I Pet. 2:24]. St. Paul says, "God has made him a sinner for us, so that through him we would be made just" [II Cor. 5:21]. You must stake everything on these and similar verses. The more your conscience torments you, the more tenaciously must you cling to them. If you do not do that, but presume to still your conscience with your contrition and penance, you will never obtain peace of mind, but will have to despair in the end. If we allow sin to remain in our conscience and try to deal with it there, or if we look at sin in our heart, it will be much too strong for us and will live on forever. But if we behold it resting on Christ and [see it] overcome by his resurrection, and then boldly believe this, even it is dead and nullified. Sin cannot remain on Christ, since it is swallowed up by his resurrection. Now you see no wounds, no pain in him, and no sign of sin. Thus St. Paul de-

---

[17] See pp. xiv-xv.
[18] Luther was often critical of pilgrimages. See, for example, in this volume, p. 40, and *LW* 44, 86-87.

clares that "Christ died for our sin and rose for our justification" [Rom. 4:25]. That is to say, in his suffering Christ makes our sin known and thus destroys it, but through his resurrection he justifies us and delivers us from all sin, if we believe this.

14. If, as was said before, you cannot believe, you must entreat God for faith. This too rests entirely in the hands of God. What we said about suffering also applies here, namely, that sometimes faith is granted openly, sometimes in secret.

However, you can spur yourself on to believe. First of all, you must no longer contemplate the suffering of Christ (for this has already done its work and terrified you), but pass beyond that and see his friendly heart and how this heart beats with such love for you that it impels him to bear with pain your conscience and your sin. Then your heart will be filled with love for him, and the confidence of your faith will be strengthened. Now continue and rise beyond Christ's heart to God's heart and you will see that Christ would not have shown this love for you if God in his eternal love had not wanted this, for Christ's love for you is due to his obedience to God. Thus you will find the divine and kind paternal heart, and, as Christ says, you will be drawn to the Father through him. Then you will understand the words of Christ, "For God so loved the world that he gave his only Son, etc." [John 3:16]. We know God aright when we grasp him not in his might or wisdom (for then he proves terrifying), but in his kindness and love. Then faith and confidence are able to exist, and then man is truly born anew in God.

15. After your heart has thus become firm in Christ, and love, not fear of pain, has made you a foe of sin, then Christ's passion must from that day on become a pattern for your entire life. Henceforth you will have to see his passion differently. Until now we regarded it as a sacrament which is active in us while we are passive, but now we find that we too must be active, namely, in the following. If pain or sickness afflicts you, consider how paltry this is in comparison with the thorny crown and the nails of Christ. If you are obliged to do or to refrain from doing things against your wishes, ponder how Christ was bound and captured and led hither and yon. If you are beset by pride, see how your Lord was mocked

and ridiculed along with criminals. If unchastity and lust assail you, remember how ruthlessly Christ's tender flesh was scourged, pierced, and beaten. If hatred, envy, and vindictiveness beset you, recall that Christ, who indeed had more reason to avenge himself, interceded with tears and cries for you and for all his enemies. If sadness or any adversity, physical or spiritual, distresses you, strengthen your heart and say, "Well, why should I not be willing to bear a little grief, when agonies and fears caused my Lord to sweat blood in the Garden of Gethsemane? He who lies abed while his master struggles in the throes of death is indeed a slothful and disgraceful servant."

So then, this is how we can draw strength and encouragement from Christ against every vice and failing. That is a proper contemplation of Christ's passion, and such are its fruits. And he who exercises himself in that way does better than to listen to every story of Christ's passion or to read all the masses. This is not to say that masses are of no value, but they do not help us in such meditation and exercise.

Those who thus make Christ's life and name a part of their own lives are true Christians. St. Paul says, "Those who belong to Christ have crucified their flesh with all its desires" [Gal. 5:24]. Christ's passion must be met not with words or forms, but with life and truth. Thus St. Paul exhorts us, "Consider him who endured such hostility from evil people against himself, so that you may be strengthened and not be weary at heart" [Heb. 12:3]. And St. Peter, "Since therefore Christ suffered in the flesh, strengthen and arm yourselves by meditating on this" [I Pet. 4:1]. However, such meditation has become rare, although the letters of St. Paul and St. Peter abound with it. We have transformed the essence into semblance and painted our meditations on Christ's passion on walls and made them into letters.[19]

---

[19] Text T, printed at Wittenberg in 1520, adds a final line: *Soli deo gloria.* WA 2, 142.

AN EXPOSITION OF THE LORD'S PRAYER FOR SIMPLE LAYMEN

1519

Translated by Martin H. Bertram

INTRODUCTION

From June, 1516, to February, 1517, Luther preached a series of sermons on the Ten Commandments, the intent of which was to help the laymen of Wittenberg to grasp the cardinal themes of Christian faith and life. This series was followed by one expounding the Lord's Prayer (Lent, 1517).[1] These sermons on the Lord's Prayer were heard, copied, and published by two of Luther's later co-workers: John Agricola and Nicholas Amsdorf. Agricola's version[2] appeared in five editions between 1518 and 1519. Amsdorf's version,[3] prepared for publication because of Luther's dissatisfaction with Agricola's, came out in May, 1519. One month before, in April, 1519, Luther's own version, which he had begun to prepare toward the end of 1518, was published.[4] Between 1519 and 1522 the Reformer's version went through thirteen editions printed at Wittenberg, Leipzig, Basel, and St. Ursula's Monastery. A Latin translation was published at Leipzig in 1520.[5]

Luther's version of the *Exposition* at once became very popular in German-speaking areas. Beatus Rhenanus was so favorably impressed by it that he expressed the hope that Luther's books, especially the *Exposition*, might find their way into every Swiss home.[6] A Venetian printer who had read the book but did not know the identity of its author was reported by John Mathesius to have exclaimed, "Blessed are the hands that wrote this. Blessed are the eyes that see it. Blessed shall be the hearts that believe this book and cry to God."[7] Of course, reaction to the book was not uniformly

---

[1] *WA* 1, 398.

[2] *Auslegung und Deutung des heiligen Vaterunsers durch den ehrwürdigen und hochgelarten Martin Luther* (*Exposition and Interpretation of the Lord's Prayer*).

[3] *Eine christliche Vorbetrachtung, so man will beten das heilige Vaterunser* (*A Christian Meditation for Anyone who Wants to Pray the Lord's Prayer*).

[4] This version reflected a subsequent series of meditations delivered to children and common people. *MA*[3], 517-518.

[5] The identity of the translator is not known. Luther had declined Spalatin's request that he prepare a Latin translation of his work. *LW* 48, 113.

[6] This sentiment was expressed in a letter to Zwingli written on July 2, 1519. See *WA* 2, 75.

[7] *WA* 2, 75.

favorable. Duke George of Saxony told Luther that the recently published book on the Lord's Prayer had confused a great many consciences.[8]

The sermons are not difficult to follow. Luther treats not just the several parts of the prayer (introduction, each of the petitions, and the Amen), but the very nature of prayer in simple terms of everyday human life.[9] The translation is based on the text, *Auslegung deutsch des Vaterunsers für die einfältigen Laien*, in WA 2, (74) 80-130.

---

[8] Duke George (1471-1539), the brother of Luther's sovereign, Elector Frederick the Wise, was an outspoken opponent of the Reformation from its very outset. The remark was made while Luther was in Leipzig for the famous debate with John Eck.

[9] See Luther's other treatments of the Lord's Prayer in *Personal Prayer Book* (1522). *LW* 43, 29-38; and *A Simple Way to Pray* (1535). *LW* 43, 194-200.

AN EXPOSITION OF THE LORD'S PRAYER FOR SIMPLE LAYMEN

Foreword

It really should not be necessary for my sermons and words to be circulated widely throughout the country. Certainly there are other books that might properly or profitably serve as sermons for the people. I do not know why God destines me to be involved in this game in which people pick up and spread my words, some as my friends, others as enemies. This has induced me to publish this Lord's Prayer, previously published by my friends,[1] and to exposit it further in the hope that I may also do my adversaries a favor. It is always my intention to be helpful to all and harmful to none.

When Christ's disciples asked him to teach them how to pray, he replied, "In praying do not heap up empty phrases as the Gentiles do; they think they will be heard for their many words. Do not be like them, for your Father in heaven knows well what you need before you ask him. Pray then like this, 'Our Father, who art in heaven, Hallowed be thy name, etc.'" [Matt. 6:7-13].

From these words of Christ we learn about both the words and the manner, that is, they tell us how and for what we are to pray. It is vital that we know both.

First, concerning the manner, that is, how we should pray. Our prayer must have few words, but be great and profound in content and meaning. The fewer the words, the better the prayer; the more words, the poorer the prayer. Few words and richness of meaning is Christian; many words and lack of meaning is pagan. Therefore Christ says that the disciples should "not heap up empty phrases

---

[1] Luther refers to the version of this work published by John Schneider, known as Agricola (cf. p. 17), whose version may be closer to Luther's original preaching than Luther's published *Exposition*. Strangely, Luther at times quotes entire sections from Agricola.

as the Gentiles do." And in John 4 [:24] he tells the Samaritan woman, "Those who worship God must pray to him in spirit and in truth." The Father desires such worshipers.

The term "to pray in spirit" or to pray spiritually is directed against untoward prayer, and the term "to pray in truth" is directed against sham prayer. For the sham oral prayer is the mouth's thoughtless mumbling and chattering. It is seen and heard by people; it is performed with the mouth, but not in truth. On the other hand, spiritual and sincere prayer reflects the heart's innermost desires, its sighing and yearning. The former makes hypocrites and gives a false sense of security; the latter makes saints and respectful children of God. However, we must make a distinction here, for external prayer springs from three different motives.

First, it may be prompted by sheer obedience, as are the prayers sung or read by priests and monks. Or, think of the prayers imposed by penance or by vows. In these, I suppose, obedience is the best part, somewhat like the obedience shown in any other physical endeavor (provided, of course, that this obedience stems from a simple sense of duty, and not for the sake of riches, honor, and praise). There is such a great measure of grace in the word of God that even a prayer that is spoken with the mouth and without devotion (with a sense of obedience) becomes fruitful and irritates the devil.

Second, a prayer may be spoken unbidden, but reluctantly and grudgingly, or for the sake of monetary reward, honor, or praise. Such a prayer were better left unspoken. However, they also receive their reward, namely, temporal goods or honors, even as God pays wages to the servants but not to the children.

Third, some prayers are spoken with devoutness of heart, but a semblance is added to the truth and the external is mingled with the internal. Yet, the inner truth breaks forth and glows with an external semblance. However, it is impossible for one who prays spiritually and sincerely to be verbose. When the soul becomes aware of what it is saying, and in its awareness tries to muster both the words and the ideas, it will be compelled to dispense with the words and cling to the thoughts, or, conversely, to lose sight of the thoughts and stress the words. Such oral prayers are to be valued only insofar as they spur and move the soul to reflect on the meaning and the desires conveyed by the words. Many psalms,[2] therefore, have captions and titles such as these: *"Ad victoriam," "Ad invitatorium,"* to indicate that these prayers, though of few words, are an invitation and inspiration to the heart to think of or to wish for something that is good. Some psalms are also distinguished by the word *Selah* (that is, rest), a word which is neither read nor sung, but exhorts us to pause and ponder when a particular item is mentioned in the prayer and to meditate on the meaning while forgetting about the words.[3]

Second, concerning the words, and what we must pray.

The words read, "Our Father, who art in heaven, etc." Since our Lord is the author of this prayer, it is without a doubt the most sublime, the loftiest, and the most excellent. If he, the good and faithful Teacher, had known a better one, he would surely have taught us that too.

This should not be misunderstood to mean that all other prayers which do not contain these words are worthless. Before Christ's birth many saints who never heard these words of Christ also prayed. What we do mean to say is that all other prayers that do not understand and express the content and meaning of this one are untrustworthy. The psalms, to be sure, are also good prayers, but although they fully embrace the main points of this prayer, they do not express them as clearly.

Therefore it is wrong to compare other prayers with this one, or even to prefer them to it, especially those with headings penned ornately in red ink,[4] in the hope alone that God will then grant good health and long life, possessions and honor, or even the remission of [temporal] punishment, and the like. Such prayers are concerned more with our honor than with God's. Thus St. Bridget's[5]

---

[2] Luther possibly is referring to the fifteen Songs of Ascent, Psalms 120 to 134.
[3] Luther's interpretation of this word is doubtful, since *Selah* is at times found in the middle of a verse (e.g., Ps. 67:1; 68:7), or at the end of a psalm (e.g., Ps. 3; 9; 24), where a pause would seem unnecessary. The word is generally regarded as an exclamation or as a directive to the musicians or the choir.
[4] Luther has in mind the ornate, private prayerbooks in wide use at that time. See *LW* 43, 5.
[5] On the Swedish St. Bridget, see *LW* 43, 12, n. 10.

fifteen prayers, rosaries, the crown prayers,[6] the Psalter, etc., have gotten the upper hand and are esteemed more highly than the Lord's Prayer. Not that I reject these prayers; I merely say that too much reliance is placed on these spoken prayers, and that consequently the truly spiritual, inner, and true Lord's Prayer is despised. For every absolution, all needs, all blessings, and all men's requirements for body and soul, for life here and beyond, are abundantly contained in that prayer. It would be better for you to pray one Lord's Prayer with a devout heart and with thought given to the words, resulting in a better life, than for you to acquire absolution through reciting all other prayers.

This prayer is divided into two parts. The first consists of a preface or introduction, the second of seven petitions.

The Introduction

Our Father, who art in heaven

The best way to begin or introduce the prayer is to know how to address, honor, and treat the person to whom we submit our petition, and how to conduct ourselves in his presence, so that he will be gracious toward us and willing to listen to us. Now, of all names there is none that gains us more favor with God than that of "Father." This is indeed a friendly, sweet, intimate, and warm-hearted word. To speak the words "Lord" or "God" or "Judge" would not be nearly as gracious and comforting to us. The name "Father" is part of our nature and is sweet by nature. That is why it is the most pleasing to God, and why no other name moves him so strongly to hear us. With this name we likewise confess that we are the children of God. which again stirs his heart mightily; for there is no lovelier sound than that of a child speaking to his father.

The words "who art in heaven" are also helpful, for they point out our miserable and pitiful condition which moves us to pray and God to have compassion on us.

---

[6] The Franciscan Crown was a seven-decade rosary, each decade of which consisted of an Our Father and ten Hail Marys. The decades honor the joys of Mary. Probably of Cistercian origin, the Crown flourished among the Friars Minor. Plenary indulgences, applicable to the dead, were attached to their use.

He who begins his prayer with the words "Our Father, who art in heaven," and does so with a sincere heart, confesses that he has a father and that this father is in heaven. He knows himself to be wretched and all alone on earth. From this must thus result a fervent yearning, like that of a child who lives far from his father's country among strangers, desolate and miserable. It says, as it were, "O Father, you are in heaven, while I, your poor child, am in misery on earth, far away from you, surrounded by many perils, in need and want, among the devils, the greatest enemies, and in much danger."

He who prays thus stands with an upright heart in the correct relationship to God; such a man is able to pray and to move God to mercy. This lofty word cannot possibly issue from human nature, but must be inspired in man's heart by the Spirit of Christ. For if we search the heart, we will discover that no man is so perfect as to be able to say truthfully that he has no father here on earth, that he possesses nothing, that he is a total stranger here, and that God is his only father. For our nature is so base that it always covets something here on earth and will not content itself with God in heaven.

The term "our Father" refers to a confidence that we can place solely in God. No other can assist us to get to heaven than this one Father. The Scriptures say, "No one ascends into heaven but he who descended from heaven, the Son of man" [John 3:13]. In his skin and on his back we too must ascend. Thus all who are heavy-laden, and even those who do not know the meaning of these words, may well pray this prayer. In fact, I regard it to be the best prayer, for then the heart says more than the lips.

Meanwhile, another person stands in church, turns the pages of his prayerbook, counts his beads, almost rattling them, while his mind wanders far from the confession of his lips. That is not praying. God says to such a one through his prophet Isaiah, "This people prays to me with their lips, but their heart is far from me" [Isa. 29:13]. Thus we also find some priests and clerics who slaver out their canonical hours[7] without heartfelt desire and still dare

---

[7] The canonical hours are the seven prayer offices, as well as the services appointed for those hours (Matins and Lauds, Prime, Terce, Sext, None, Vespers, and Compline) recited daily by priests.

to say unabashed, "Well, now I am happy. I have now settled my account with our Lord," and think that they have thereby satisfied God.

But I tell you, admitting that you may have satisfied the precepts of the church, that God will one day say to you, "This people prays to me with their lips, but their heart is far from me" [Isa. 29:13; Matt. 15:8]. It is to be feared that they will rely on such a prayer and never again direct a prayer to God. Thus those who pray least seem to pray most, and, conversely, those who pray most seem to pray least.

Nowadays we place our trust and confidence in much babbling,[8] in clamouring in songs, though Christ forbade this when he said, "No one will be heard just because he uses many words" [Matt. 6:7]. Such praying is not heard. This situation is due to the inept sermons which do not, as our dear fathers did in times past, direct the people diligently and studiously to genuine and sincere prayer of the heart, but only to a semblance of prayer, to oral prayer, and particularly to prayer for selfish gain.

Someone may say, "In Luke 18 [:1] it is written that you are to pray without ceasing." I reply: Look closely at the words. Christ does not say that you must turn pages, count beads, make many words, and the like without ceasing, but he says, "You should pray without ceasing." But as to what prayer is, we have said enough above. There have been heretics, called Euchit[9]—that is, people who prayed, who wanted to abide by the word of Christ and to pray (that is, they prattled with their mouth) day and night. This they did to the exclusion of everything else, entirely unaware of their folly, for while eating, drinking, or sleeping, they had to discontinue their prayers. Therefore Christ spoke of spiritual prayer, which may be carried on without interruption, even during physical labors, though, to be sure, no one ever accomplishes this perfectly either. Who is able to lift up his heart to God continuously? These words

---

[8] For Luther's criticism of current prayer practices, see his *Treatise on Good Works* (1520). *LW* 44, 58-60.

[9] This prayer movement stemmed from Eastern monasticism in the fifth century. Convinced that the sacraments and asceticism did not suffice for salvation, its adherents engaged in constant prayer. They were persecuted as heretics by the official church.

set a goal toward which we must strive. And when we see that we fall short of it, we must acknowledge that we are weak and frail human beings, be humbled, and plead for mercy because of our frailty.

All teachers of the Scriptures conclude that prayer is nothing else than the lifting up of heart or mind to God. But if the lifting up of the heart constitutes the essence and nature of prayer, it follows that everything else which does not invite the lifting of the heart is not prayer. Therefore, singing, talking, and whistling, when devoid of the sincere uplifting of the heart, are as unlike prayer as scarecrows in the garden are unlike human beings. The essence is wanting; only the appearance and name are present.

This is borne out by a story told by St. Jerome about a holy father named Agathon.[10] This man, living in the desert, carried a stone in his mouth for thirty years to teach him silence. But how did he pray? Without a doubt inwardly with his heart, which, after all, appeals to God more than anything else. In fact, it is the one mode of praying that God regards and seeks. It is, admittedly, helpful to hear the words, for they stimulate thought and true prayer. As was said before, the spoken words have no other purpose than that of a trumpet, a drum, or an organ, or any other sound which will move the heart and lift it upward to God.

Indeed, no one should depend on his heart and presume to pray without uttering words unless he is well trained in the Spirit and has experience in warding off stray thoughts. Otherwise the devil will thoroughly trick him and soon smother the prayer in his heart. Therefore we should cling to the words and with their help soar upward, until our feathers grow and we can fly without the help of words. I do not condemn words or the spoken prayer, nor should anyone spurn them. On the contrary, they are to be accepted as an especially great gift of God. However, it is wrong when the words are not employed for their fruitful purpose, namely, to move the heart, but are only mumbled and muttered with the mouth, on

---

[10] St. Jerome (347-420), one of the four great doctors of the Western church, translated the Bible into the Latin Vulgate and wrote Bible commentaries. Agricola's version adds the words: ". . . in the book which he [Jerome] wrote about those who lived a secluded life," probably the *Lives of the Hermits*. Agathon may have been the fourth-century abbot of an Egyptian hermitage.

the false assumption that this is all that is necessary. Not only is there no fruitful improvement, there is a corrupting of the heart.

Moreover, let everyone beware when he feels a little spark of devotion as he recites the words lest he fall victim to the venom of the old serpent, namely, deadly arrogance, which says, "Look! Now I am praying with heart and lips and feel such great devotion that I doubt whether there is anyone else who acquits himself as well as I do." These thoughts are inspired by the devil, and so you become worse than all those who never pray at all. Yes, such thoughts are almost like blaspheming and cursing God. You should praise not yourself, but God, in everything good that you have and feel.

Finally, we must note how precisely Christ words this prayer. He does not want anyone to pray only for himself, but for all mankind. He does not teach us to say "My Father," but "Our Father." Since prayer is a spiritual good which is held in common by all, we dare not deprive anyone of it, not even our enemies. For since God is the Father of us all, he also wants us to be like brothers to each other, who love each other dearly and who pray for one another as each does for himself.

Division of the Lord's Prayer

We find seven petitions in this prayer.

The first petition:
Hallowed be Thy name

The second petition:
Thy kingdom come.

The third petition:
Thy will be done, as it is in heaven.

The fourth petition:
Give us this day our daily bread.

The fifth petition:
And forgive us our trespasses, as we forgive those who trespass against us.

The sixth petition:
And lead us not into temptation.

The seventh petition:
But deliver us from evil.

These petitions may well also be termed seven good lessons and exhortations. For as the holy bishop and martyr St. Cyprian[11] suggests, they are seven reminders of our wretchedness and poverty by means of which man, led to a knowledge of self, can see what a miserable and perilous life he leads here on earth. Such a life is nothing but blasphemy of God's name, disobedience to his will, rejection of his kingdom, a hungry land without bread, an existence full of sin, a precarious sojourn, and an abounding in every evil. As we shall see later, Christ himself talks of them in this prayer.

The First Petition

Hallowed be thy name

Though of but few words, what an infinitely profound petition this is if prayed from the heart! Among the seven petitions there is none greater for us to pray than, "Hallowed be thy name." But note that God's name is holy in itself and is not hallowed by us, for it is God who hallows us and all things. No, this means (as St. Cyprian declares) that it must be hallowed in us.[12] In this petition God becomes everything and man becomes nothing. The other six petitions serve the same purpose and intent, namely, the hallowing of God's name. If that is done, then everything is done well, as we shall see.

To see how God's name is hallowed in us, we first ask how it is profaned and dishonored in us. To clarify this, we say bluntly that it is dishonored in us in a twofold manner: first, when we misuse God's name for the purpose of sinning; second, when we steal and rob him of this name. A holy vessel in church may be desecrated similarly in a twofold manner: first, when it is not used in the service of God but for human purposes; second, if it is robbed and stolen.

---

[11] Cyprian, a pagan rhetorician, was converted to Christianity in 246. As bishop of Carthage he suffered a martyr's death in 258. The writing of Cyprian which Luther has in mind is probably *On the Lord's Prayer*.
[12] *On the Lord's Prayer*, 12.

The name of God is first profaned in us when we misuse it, as, for instance, when we employ it, not for the care, betterment, or benefit of our soul, but for sinful ends and the detriment of our soul. The various ways in which this is done are, for instance, witchcraft, exorcism, lying, swearing, cursing, deceiving. These are all included in God's second commandment: "Thou shalt not take the name of the Lord thy God in vain." Briefly summed up, we profane God's name when we do not live as his children.

What the children of God are like

We call a child devout who is born of upright parents, who obeys and is like them in every respect. Such a child rightfully possesses and inherits property and the full name of his parents. Thus we Christians, through our rebirth in baptism, became children of God. And if we pattern ourselves after our Father and all his ways, all his goods and names are likewise our inheritance forever. Now, our Father is and is called merciful and good, as Christ says, "Be merciful, even as your Father is merciful" [Luke 6:36]. He also says, "Learn from me; for I am gentle and lowly in heart" [Matt. 11:29]. God is, furthermore, just, pure, truthful, strong, guileless, wise, etc. These are all names of God and are comprehended in the words "thy name," for the names of all virtues are also names given to God. And since we are baptized into these names and are consecrated and hallowed by them, and since they have thus become our names, it follows that God's children should be called and also be gentle, merciful, chaste, just, truthful, guileless, friendly, peaceful, and kindly disposed toward all, even toward our enemies. For the name of God, in which we were baptized, works all this in us. But we should always pray that the name of God may abide in us, be active in us, and be hallowed.

But whoever is wrathful, quarrelsome, envious, rancorous, unkind, unmerciful, unchaste, who curses, lies, swears, defrauds, and slanders, that person truly defiles, blasphemes, and profanes the divine name in which he was blessed, baptized, or called, numbered among Christians, and gathered into the congregation of God. Such a person actually honors the devil's name under the guise of honoring the name of God, for that one is a liar, a backbiter, impure, hateful, etc. And, as we read in the Wisdom of Solomon [2:24], "Those who are his kith and kin follow him." Really, people like those are like a priest who would let a sow drink from the sacred chalice or ladle out putrid manure with it. So these people place their body and soul, in which the name of God dwells and with which they are hallowed, in the service of the devil. Thus the holy and divine name in which they were consecrated is now desecrated.

See, now you understand the meaning of the term "to hallow" and "holy." It is nothing else than withdrawing something from misuse and dedicating it to its proper godly use, just as a church is dedicated and appointed solely to the service of God. In like manner we must be hallowed in our whole life, leaving nothing but the name of God to dwell in us, in other words, nothing but kindness, truth, justice, etc. Hence the name of God is hallowed or profaned not only with our lips but also with our soul and all the members of our body.

Second, God's name is defiled by robbing and thieving. Although wise men will at once understand what I mean, it will be too subtle for the simpleminded, since we are here referring to the arrogant ones who regard themselves as righteous and holy and do not feel that they are profaning the name of God as those in the aforementioned group do. While they dub themselves righteous and holy and truthful, they freely and fearlessly pilfer and purloin God's name. There are a very great many such persons today, especially when one thinks that they are pious and respectful people. They have a high opinion of themselves, they take pride in their words, their deeds, their wisdom and ability, demanding honor and recognition for them. If these are withheld, they rave and rage angrily. In the Scriptures they are characterized as *profundi corde*, as of a profound heart, so that God alone can penetrate and understand them. It causes him much trouble. They can embellish everything so cleverly that they themselves are duped into thinking that all is completely right with them. Their self-complacency, inward boasting, bragging, and self-praise are their greatest and most perilous handicap. We shall discuss further how we can recognize them and how to preserve ourselves from a like misfortune.

The worst and most harmful people in Christendom

In the first place, they constantly use the word "always." They boast and say, "Oh, I am so good at heart; I mean so well. Such and such a person refuses to follow me, though I am willing to share my very heart with him." Be on your guard, beware of these wolves who walk in such sheep's clothing [Matt. 7:15]. They are hedges which bear not figs, but only thorns [Matt. 7:16]. Of them Christ says, "You will know them by their fruits" [Matt. 7:20]. And what are their fruits? Not good words and deeds, but stabbing, stinging, scratching, gouging, and wounding. And how do they do that? Note well that it happens when these people become convinced of their piety, when they have a good opinion of themselves, when they discover that they pray more, fast more, and perform other good works more and that they are endowed by God with more understanding and grace than other people. They do not dare to compare themselves with persons who are higher and better but with those who seem to be less and worse than they. They soon forget that everything they have is a gift from God. Now this is bound to lead to judging, condemning, slandering, backbiting, despising others. Thus they strut in their arrogance, becoming hard-hearted and devoid of all fear of God. In fact, all they do is fill and befoul their heart and lips with the sins of others.

See, their fruits are thistles and thorns. Here are the maws of wolves disguised in sheep's clothing.

Now you see that that is what is meant by stealing God's name and honor and ascribing these to oneself. God alone has the right to pass judgment, as Christ says, "Judge not, that you be not judged" [Matt. 7:1]. Furthermore, God's name alone is holy, righteous, and good. We all are sinners before God, one as well as the other, without any distinction. And if anyone should be superior to another, he cannot take credit for this, for it is of God. If he is to have a name, good will, praise, and esteem, these must be given to him by others. Hence, he who uses the name, not for his neighbor's benefit, but in contempt of him, robs God of his honor, usurps God's honor, and arrogates to himself the nature and virtue which are God's and not his.

Today the world is full of these pernicious, insolent, vile, and ungodly spirits who blaspheme God's name more shamefully with their respectable lives than all others do with their evil lives. Those who would be better than other people, like the hypocrite in the Gospel [Luke 18:11], I call arrogant saints and the devil's martyrs. Blind to their own evil and sinfulness, they disdain the sinners and the unrighteous and will have nothing to do with them, lest people say, "Does he associate with such people? I had surely thought he was much more pious." They do not understand that God granted them more grace than others so that they might serve others with this grace, and that they should increase and share with others. That is to say, they were to pray for others, help them, counsel them, and do unto others as God did to them. After all, God did not judge them with scorn but gave them this grace as a free gift. However, they go their way and not only prevent this grace from bearing fruit, but even use it to persecute the very ones they should help with it. These are the ones the Scriptures call *perversos*. In Psalm 18 [:26] we read, *"Cum perverso perveteris"* ["with the perverse thou art perverse"]. Furthermore, when these people hear that God alone is worthy of name and honor they put on a nice act and deceive themselves still more with their hypocrisy, saying that in all they do they strive only for God's honor, protesting and probably swearing that they do not seek their own honor. So thoroughly and profoundly, yes, even spiritually, depraved are they!

But now note their fruits and their deeds. When they are thwarted in their projects, you will hear them wail and wonder why no one can get along with them. They claim that those who hinder them are wrong. They cannot forget that hurt, claiming meanwhile that God's honor was impeded and that the people resisted the good cause which they intended to promote. They cannot refrain from their accursed judging and slander. Thus one can see their true intent and that they are not wroth because a good cause and God's honor were obstructed, but because their own opinion and plans did not prevail. They act as though their own opinion could not be otherwise than good, in fact, so good that God himself would not repudiate it. If they were not so sure about their own good, they would not object when they are hindered. However, arrogance does not want to be judged as evil or foolish. Therefore, in their eyes,

31

all others are evil and foolish. Just see how deeply their blasphemy of God is imbedded in these spirits who would claim to be and to have that which is God's alone, namely, wisdom, justice, name, and honor.

In the third place, when they hear it said and proclaimed that God alone is entitled to name and honor because he created and owns everything, they pose as more learned than all preachers, even than the Holy Spirit. They think they teach everyone and need learn from no one, saying, "Oh, who does not know that?" implying that they already knew it. But when it comes to the point that their own honor is questioned, that people esteem them lightly or even despise them, deprive them of something, or that they meet with reverses, then, lo and behold, their virtues soon vanish; then the thorny thicket bears its fruit: prickly thorns. Then the donkey with its ears peeps out through the lion's skin. Then they moan, "O God in heaven, look down and see how greatly we are wronged!" They even commit the great folly of saying that they have been wronged even before God.

What happened to your great intelligence which once allowed you to say that all things come from the hand of God and are his? O wretched man! If they are God's alone, why should he not have the right to give them and take them without your interference, to toss them back and forth? If all things are his, you ought to keep your peace and let God administer all as he wishes. If he takes that which belongs to him, he is not dealing unjustly with you. Thus the saintly Job said after he had lost his children and all his property, "The Lord gave it, and the Lord has taken it away; blessed be the name of the Lord" [Job 1:21]. Job, indeed, was a just man from whom no one could take anything because he had nothing that he called his own. God declares in Job 41 [:11], "Whatever is under the heaven is mine; I created it." Why, then, do you boast about your possessions and wail about an injustice done you? If anyone touches your honor, your reputation, your possessions, or anything else that you have, he is encroaching not upon what is yours, but what is Christ's. And to drive this lesson home to you, God ordains that all that be taken from you which you assumed was yours so that you may realize that it is not yours, but his. So then, we always

32

see that people do not really seek God's name and honor, especially those haughty saints who aspire to be and have something which belongs only to God.

Now you may say, "If that is true, then it follows that no one on earth hallows God's name satisfactorily; furthermore, all those who have court dealings touching on property or honor or other things do wrong."

I reply first of all: That is why I just called this first petition an unlimited one, the foremost one, encompassing all the others. If anyone were able to hallow God's name perfectly, he would no longer need to pray the Lord's Prayer. If anyone were so holy that he was no longer concerned with his own honor or with any possessions, he would be holy indeed and the name of God would be perfectly hallowed in him. Such a person, however, does not belong to this earth, but only to heaven. Therefore we ought to pray and to plead as long as we live that God may hallow his name in us. All men are blasphemers of God's name, some to a greater, others to a lesser degree, even though the arrogant saints refuse to believe this.

For that reason I also said that this prayer is not only a petition but also a wholesome lesson and an indicator of our wretched and accursed life on earth, humbling man in his own esteem. Now when we pray that God's name may be hallowed in us, this implies that it is not yet holy in us; if it were, we would not have to pray for it. This implies further that we, during our lifetime, defile, blaspheme, dishonor, profane, and desecrate God's name. We testify with our own prayer and with our mouth that we are blasphemers of God.

In all the Scriptures I know of no other passage that denounces and dooms our life more than this petition. Who is there who would not want to die soon with loathing of this life (even though he otherwise does love God's name) when he realizes in his heart that his life consists basically of profaning God's name and honor? Furthermore, anyone who has a thorough understanding of the Lord's Prayer, and only that, would be equipped with doctrine sufficient to combat all vices, especially that of pride. How can that man remain happy and proud who confesses in the Lord's Prayer so many great and horrible sins in himself, for instance, that he dishonors

God's name, daily violates the Second Commandment, and uses God's name in vain?

In the second place, I ˌ ˙˙ that it is best not to engage in lawsuits. It would be better if there were none. However, to forestall greater evils and as a favor to those who are not yet able to surrender all and return it again to God, such suits are permitted to those who are still imperfect. Nevertheless, a goal has been set for us toward which we must work. That is to say, we must learn from day to day and exercise ourselves in giving up and returning to God his name, honor, goods, and all things. In this way we become perfectly hallowed. This petition has been given us so that our hearts may unceasingly yearn to have God's name hallowed.

It should really not surprise a Christian if he were to be deprived of everything—of property, honor, friends, health, wisdom, etc., for ultimately the day must come when all his possessions are destroyed and he is separated from them all—before he is hallowed and before he hallows the name of God. For as long as something remains, a name will also remain. Therefore everything must be removed so that only God, all things of God and all his names, remain. Then the righteous will be, as the Scriptures[13] say of them, poor and orphaned, deprived of their parents, and without solace.

But you may say, "If we all fall short of honoring God's name, do we thereby commit a mortal and damning sin?" I reply: This would indeed be a mortal and damning sin if God were to deal severely with us, for God cannot tolerate even the slightest sin. However, there are two kinds of people. There are some who recognize and deplore that they do not fully hallow God's name, who earnestly pray that they may do so, and who take seriously their wretchedness. To them God grants what they ask. And because they judge and condemn themselves, he absolves them and remits their shortcomings. The others, those unthinking and frivolous spirits who make light of their failings, throw them to the winds, or do not even see them, and who never pray, will in the end discover how great the sin was to which they closed their eyes. They will be damned for the very thing which they supposed would most

---

[13] In a general way Luther possibly is referring to passages such as Matt. 11:5; Luke 6:20; II Cor. 6:10; Jas. 2:5.

surely save them, for Christ says to the hypocrites that they will receive the greater condemnation because of their long prayers [Matt. 23:14].

Now see how the Lord's Prayer teaches you first of all to recognize your great misery and corruption as a blasphemer of God. Consequently, you must be terrified by your own prayer when you realize what you are praying. For it must be true that you still have not hallowed God's name. It must then be equally true that he who fails to hallow God's name profanes it. It must be true, furthermore, that the profaning of God's name is a grave sin and deserving of eternal hellfire if God's justice were to prevail. What, then, do you propose to do? Your own prayer reproves you and turns against you; it accuses you and bears witness against you. There you lie! Who will help you?

See then, if you have earnestly repented, if you are really humbled by the recognition of your wretchedness, then there comes the comforting teaching that will lift you up again. That is to say, this petition also teaches you not to despair, but to ask for God's grace and help. For you must be certain and firmly believe that God taught you to pray like this because he intended to grant your prayer to you. Thus the result of the prayer is that God does not count your sin against you and does not deal harshly with you. God looks with favor only on those who sincerely confess that they dishonor his name and ever desire that it may be hallowed.

On the other hand, those who trust in their conscience and do not believe that they are dishonoring God's name cannot be saved. They are still too sure and secure, too haughty; they do not stand in awe of God. They do not belong to those to whom Christ says, "Come to me, all who labor and are heavy-laden, and I will give you rest" [Matt. 11:28]. They do not understand the Lord's Prayer and do not hear what they are praying.

Summary

This is the sum and substance of this petition: O dear Father, may your name be hallowed in us; that is, I confess and am sorry that I have dishonored your name so often and that in my arrogance I still defile your name by honoring my own. Therefore, help me by your grace so that I and my name become nothing, so that only you and your name and honor may live in me.

I hope that you have also fully understood that the term "your name" is the equivalent of "your honor" or "your praise." The Scriptures equate a good name with honor and praise, and a bad name with disgrace and ill repute. This petition, then, demands nothing else than that God's honor be sought in all, before all, and beyond all else, and that our whole life redound forever only to God's glory. Our life should not be directed toward our own advantage, not even to our salvation or any blessing, whether temporal or eternal, unless all of this ultimately leads to God's honor and praise.

So this is the first petition. For by honoring God we bring him the first and the last and the highest offering within our power; nor does he seek and ask for more. Moreover, we cannot give God anything else, for it is he who gives us everything else. But he does claim for himself this honor, namely, that we acknowledge and witness in our words and songs, our lives and deeds, in all that we do and suffer, that everything is of God, in support of Psalm 111 [:3], "*Confessio et magnificentia opus eius,*" "Full of honor and majesty is his work, and his righteousness endures forever." That is to say, the deeds of him in whom God lives and works do nothing else but accord God great honor and glory and ascribe all to him. Hence, such a person will not be disturbed when dishonor and contempt are heaped on him, for he knows that it is right. And if no one else wants to dishonor and despise him, he will do this himself. He dislikes being lauded and exalted. In that respect he is just, giving to God what is God's and to himself what is his, to God honor and everything else, to himself dishonor and nothing else. That is the justice that endures forever for it appeals not only to man here in time—such as the lamps of the foolish virgins and the righteousness of sham saints[14]—but also to the eternal God, with whom justice abides forever.

Now you observe that this petition contends against this accursed arrogance, which is the head and the life and the essence of all sins. Just as no virtue can have its being and be accounted good when tainted with this arrogance, so no sin can live or harm

---

[14] Cf. Matt. 25:1-13.

when this arrogance is dead. Just as a serpent has all its life in its head—that being dead, the serpent cannot work anyone harm—even so all sins are harmless, yes, even very beneficial, when arrogance is destroyed. Hence, since no one is without pride, and since everyone covets his own name and honor, there can be no one for whom this petition is not very necessary and useful.

The Second Petition

Thy kingdom come

The second petition, like the others, does two things: it humbles us and it raises us up. It humbles us because it compels us with our own lips to confess our great and pitiable misery. But it raises us up because it shows us how to conduct ourselves in such abasement. Every word of God terrifies and comforts us, hurts and heals; it breaks down and builds up; it plucks up and plants again; it humbles and exalts [Jer. 1:10].

In the first place, this petition humbles us when we openly admit that God's kingdom has not yet come to us. When earnestly pondered and deeply sought, this is frightening and will surely appall and aggrieve any pious heart. For we must infer from this petition that we are still rejected, that we are in misery and among cruel foes, robbed of our dearest Father's land.

This leads to two distressing and woeful losses. The first is that God the Father is robbed of his kingdom in us, and that he who is and should be Lord over all is blocked in his power and title only by us. This dishonors him greatly, since it makes him a lord without a land and his title of omnipotence becomes an object of ridicule in us. That thought must undoubtedly distress all who love God and wish him well. Furthermore, it is terrible that we are the ones who impair and obstruct God's kingdom. And if he were to deal justly with us, he might very well condemn us as enemies and despoilers of his kingdom.

The other loss is our own. It consists in this, that we are wretched captives of powerful foes in strange lands. It is terrible and lamentable when an earthly prince's child or a whole country is held captive by the Turks,[15] subjected to shame and suffering, and finally suffers the most horrible death, but it is far more lamentable that we lie in this misery among the evil spirits, exposed to all sorts of dangers to body and soul, and expect eternal death at any moment. When seen rightly, we might well shudder more at the thought of our own life than at that of a hundred deaths.

In the second place, when such a thought has abased us and shown us our misery, solace is quick to follow. The kind teacher, our Lord Jesus, instructs us to pray and petition for rescue from our misery and not to despair. Those who confess that they impede God's kingdom and pray sorrowfully that this kingdom might still come to them, will, because of their penitence and prayer, be pardoned by God, when he would otherwise rightly punish them. But, together with the tyrants and the destroyers of his kingdom, he will surely and severely judge those brazen spirits who are indifferent to the state of the kingdom and who do not earnestly pray for it. Since everyone is bound to pray this petition, it follows that no one is guiltless with regard to God's kingdom. To understand this is to know that there are two kingdoms.

The first kingdom is a kingdom of the devil. In the Gospel the Lord calls the devil a prince or king of this world [John 16:11], that is, of a kingdom of sin and disobedience. To the godly, however, that kingdom is nothing but misery and a vast prison, as we find foreshown in times past in the sojourn of the children of Israel in Egypt. They were compelled to cultivate the land, to toil and suffer much woe, yet they gained nothing but the death that was planned for them [Exod. 1:10-16]. Thus he who submissively serves the devil in sin must suffer much, especially in his conscience, and yet, in the end, he will thereby earn nothing but everlasting death.

Now, all of us dwell in the devil's kingdom until the coming of the kingdom of God. However, there is a difference. To be sure, the godly are also in the devil's kingdom, but they daily and steadfastly contend against sins and resist the lusts of the flesh, the allurements of the world, the whisperings of the devil. After all, no matter how godly we may be, the evil lust always wants to share the reign

---

[15] By this time the Muslim Turks had conquered the Near East and also Bosnia (1463), Albania (1466), and Syria and Egypt (1517).

in us and would like to rule us completely and overcome us. In that way God's kingdom unceasingly engages in combat with the devil's kingdom. And the members of the former are preserved and saved because they, within themselves, fight against the devil's kingdom in order to enlarge the kingdom of God. It is they who pray this petition with words, hearts, and deeds. Thus the holy apostle Paul says that "we must not let sin reign in our mortal bodies, to make us obey its passions" [Rom. 6:12]. He says as it were: You will indeed have and feel evil lusts, a love of and inclination to anger, greed, unchastity, and the like, all of which would lure you into the devil's kingdom, that is, into sin. These emotions issue out of that same kingdom and are sins in themselves. However, you must not give way to them, but fight against them and forcibly subdue these traitors left behind from the old kingdom of the devil, just as the children of Israel did with the Jebusites and Amorites [II Sam. 5:6-7]. In that way you increase the kingdom of God—that is, the true promised land—in you.

The others dwell in this kingdom, enjoy it, and freely do the bidding of the flesh, the world, and the devil. If they could, they would always stay there. They yield to the devil; they impair, yes, devastate God's kingdom. To that end they amass goods, build magnificent houses, and covet all that the world can bestow, just as though they wanted to remain here forever. They do not pause to consider that as St. Paul says "here we have no lasting city" [Heb. 13:14]. These people utter this prayer with their lips, but contradict it with their hearts. They are like lead organ pipes which fairly drawl or shout out their sounds in church, yet lack both words and meaning. Perhaps these organs represent and symbolize these singers and petitioners.

The other kingdom is that of God, namely, a kingdom of truth and righteousness, of which Christ says, "Seek first the kingdom of God and his righteousness" [Matt. 6:33]. What is God's or his kingdom's righteousness? It is the state when we are free from sin, when all our members, talents, and powers are subject to God and are employed in his service, enabling us to say with Paul, "I live, but it is no longer I but Christ who lives in me" [Gal. 2:20]. To the Corinthians he said, "You are not your own; you were bought with

39

a price. So glorify and bear God in your body" [I Cor. 6:19-20]. He says as it were: Christ bought you with his very self. Therefore, you must be his and let him live and reign in you. That comes to pass when we are ruled not by sin, but only by Christ and his grace. Thus God's kingdom consists only of peace, discipline, humility, chastity, love, and every other virtue, and is devoid of wrath, hatred, bitterness, unchastity, and every other vice.

Now let everyone test himself to see whether he is inclined in this or in that direction, and he will know to which kingdom he belongs. There is, of course, no one who will not find some trace of the devil's kingdom in himself. Therefore he must pray, "Thy kingdom come." For God's kingdom does indeed begin and grow here, but it will be perfected in yonder life.

Thus the petition "Thy kingdom come" briefly declares this: "Dear Father, do not let us sojourn very long here on earth, so that your kingdom may be consummated in us and we may be delivered completely from the devil's kingdom. But if it pleases you to let us linger longer in this misery, grant us your grace that we may begin to build and constantly to increase your kingdom in us, but reduce and destroy the devil's kingdom."

Now note that two great errors are involved in this matter. The first is committed by those who run hither and yon for the purpose of becoming righteous, of entering God's kingdom, and of being saved. The one runs to Rome, the other to St. James;[16] one builds a chapel, another donates this, still another one that. However, they refuse to face the true issue, that is, they will not give their inmost self to God and thus become his kingdom. They perform many outward works which glitter very nicely, but inwardly they remain full of malice, anger, hatred, pride, impatience, unchastity, etc.

It is against them that Christ spoke when he was asked when the kingdom of God was coming, "The kingdom of God does not come with outward signs or appearances; for behold, the kingdom of God is within you" [Luke 17:20-21]. Christ also says in Matthew

---

[16] St. James (Santiago) Church of Campostela in northwestern Spain, frequently mentioned by Luther, was purportedly the site of the missionary labors, martyr's death, and burial of St. James the Elder. It was one of the most famous places of pilgrimage during the Middle Ages.

24 [:23-24], "If anyone says to you, 'Lo, here it is!' or 'There it is!' do not believe it. For false prophets will arise." He means to say: If you want to know the kingdom of God, do not go far afield in search of it. If you wish to have it, you will find it close to you. Yes, it is not only close to you, it is in you. For decency, humility, truthfulness, chastity, and all other virtues (these make up the true kingdom of God) one cannot fetch from across the land or the sea. They must blossom in the heart.

Therefore we do not pray, "Dear Father, let us come into your kingdom," as though we might journey toward it. But we do say, "May thy kingdom come to us." If we are to receive it at all, God's grace and his kingdom, together with all virtues, must come to us. We will never be able to come into this kingdom. Similarly, Christ came to us from heaven to earth; we did not ascend from earth into heaven to him.

The other error made by many who pray this petition is to think of nothing but their own eternal bliss. They suppose that the kingdom of God is composed of sheer joy and happiness in heaven. Inspired by their carnal sense and by their dread of hell, they seek only their own benefit and advantage in heaven. These people are unaware that God's kingdom consists of nothing other than piety, decency, purity, gentleness, kindness, and of every other virtue and grace; they do not know that God must have his way in us, that he alone must be, dwell, and reign in us. We must strive for that goal first and foremost. We are saved only when God reigns in us and we are his kingdom. We need not seek, desire, or pray for joy and happiness and all other desirable things, for they will all be ours when his kingdom comes. A good wine will naturally and inevitably produce joy and happiness when it is drunk. Even more, when grace and virtue (that is, the kingdom of God) are perfected, they result in joy and peace and bliss, and in every delight, naturally and surely and without our aid. Therefore, to turn our eyes away from false and selfish goals, Christ bids us to seek and to ask for God's kingdom itself and not for the fruits of the kingdom. Those people, however, begin at the far end and seek first that which should be last, meanwhile neglecting the first or valuing it solely because of the ultimate fruit. Consequently, they will receive nothing at all. They

41

do not desire that which comes first, and therefore that which follows will not be theirs either.

The Third Petition

Thy will be done on earth, as it is in heaven

This petition has the same twofold effect as the preceding one, that is, it humbles and it exalts; it makes sinners and it makes righteous people; for the Word of God always works both judgment and righteousness. We read, "Blessed are they who practice justice and righteousness at all times" [Ps. 106:3]. Judgment consists of nothing else but that man recognizes his condition and judges and condemns himself. That is true humility and self-abasement. Righteousness is nothing else but recognition of self, followed by a plea and petition for God's mercy and help by which a man is then exalted before God. We shall study these two points in this petition.

In the first place, we judge and accuse ourselves with our own words, declaring that we are disobedient to God and do not do his will. For if we really did his will, this petition would not be necessary. It is really frightening to hear ourselves say, "Thy will be done." What can be more terrible than our own frank admission in this petition that God's will is not being done and that his commandment is disdained. If we pray in this manner, it is obviously true that we are not doing and have not done God's will. In God's sight sham and hypocrisy avail nothing, for we must pray in accord with the facts as they really are.

Since we find it necessary to pray this petition until our death, it follows that we are also found to be guilty of disobedience to God's will until our end. Who, in the face of our conviction by our own prayer, could be so arrogant as to deny that if God were to deal with us according to his justice, he should reasonably condemn us at any time for the disobedience which we have confessed with our own lips? So then, this petition brings about genuine humility and a fear of God and his judgment, and we are happy to escape God's judgment and to be saved by pure mercy and grace. To know oneself thoroughly and to bemoan one's condition means, as this petition shows, to condemn oneself and to pass judgment on oneself before God.

In the second place, righteousness consists of this, that having known and judged ourselves, we do not despair before God's judgment seat, before which we plead guilty in this petition, but that we seek refuge in God's mercy and firmly trust that he will deliver us from our disobedience to his will. He who humbly confesses his disobedience and sin, who admits that he deserves the sentence and sincerely asks God for mercy, not doubting that it will be granted, is righteous before God. Thus the Apostle teaches that a person will be justified before God solely by reason of his faith and trust in God, and not because of his own works. The mercy of God is the only source of his comfort and confidence (Romans 1; Galatians 3).[17]

What a hard rebuff this petition is to our fleeting and wretched life, marking it as nothing but disobedience to the divine will and thus as a sure stage of eternal damnation. It asserts that our life is preserved only by our admission of this, by our lament over it, and by our fervent plea for it. He who reflects deeply on this and the other petitions can truly have but little love for this life. He who does love such a life betrays that he does not in the least understand the Lord's Prayer or the perils of his life.

What does it mean to say that God's will is done, or that it is not done? That God's will be done means undoubtedly nothing else than that his commandments are kept, for through these God has revealed his will to us. Here it is necessary to know and to understand God's commandments. This is a very broad statement. Briefly stated, it refers to distinguishing the old self, the old Adam in us, as the holy Apostle teaches us in many passages (for example, Romans 6 [:6]). The old Adam is simply the evil leaning in us toward wrath, hatred, unchastity, greed, vainglory, pride, and the like. These evil impulses were inherited from Adam and born in us through our mothers. From these stem all kinds of evil deeds such

---

[17] Rom. 1:17 and Gal. 3:11 are basic to Luther's Reformation concepts. Cf. *WA, TR* 3, 3232c; *LW* 54, 193-194 (No. 3232c). Cf. also the *Lectures on Galatians*, which Luther was readying for print at this time. *LW* 27, 257-258.

as murder, adultery, robbery, and similar transgressions of God's commandments, which cannot happen without disobedience to God's will.

The old Adam is mortified in two ways so that God's will may be done. In the first place, he is mortified by us when we subdue and suppress our base impulses, when we restrain our unchastity by fasting, watching, prayer, and labor, when we undo our neighbor's hatred and ill will by alms and other acts of kindness, in short, when we break our own will in every way. When a person is without a teacher and master, he must learn to do not what his own will wants him to do, but always to do what runs counter to his will. He must always work against his own will. He must be firmly convinced that his will is not good, no matter how pleasant it may seem. Unless the will has been trained and guided it is better to forego doing its bidding. As I have already said, if a good will dwelt in us, we would not need this petition.

A person should learn to know a will which is superior to his and which is opposed to his own. He will never feel uncertain when he finds this one will, knowing that in him these wills are not in conflict with one another, when he accustoms himself to follow the superior will rather than his own. He who has and obeys his own will surely acts contrary to God's will. But as it happens, there is nothing so dear to man and so hard to surrender as his own will. Many people perform fine and good works, but they completely follow their own will and inclinations, assuming all the time that all is well and that they are not doing wrong. They are of the opinion that their will is good and true and that they do not in the least need this petition. They are also without any fear of God.

In the second place, this petition mortifies us through other people who antagonize us, assail us, disquiet us, and oppose our will in every way, who mock not only our worldly actions but also our good spiritual works, such as our prayers, our fasting, our acts of kindness, who, in brief, are never at peace with us. O what a priceless blessing this is! We should really pay such assailants all our goods, for they are the ones who fulfil this petition in us. They are the ones through whom God breaks our will so that his will may be done. This is why Christ says in Matthew 5 [:25], "Make friends quickly with your accuser." That is, we must surrender our will and accept our adversary's will as good, for in that way our will is broken. In the breaking of our will God's will is done; for he wants to see our will hindered and broken. Therefore, if someone wants to reproach you or make a fool of you, do not oppose him, but say yes to him, deeming it right before God to do so, which, as a matter of fact, it is. If he wants to rob you of anything and work you harm, let him do it as though it were your just desert, for undoubtedly in God's sight it is just. Even if your adversary is doing wrong thereby, you nevertheless are not suffering an injustice, for since everything belongs to God, it is his right to take it from you either through a good or an evil person. Your will must not resist, but must say, "Thy will be done." This applies to all things, physical and spiritual. Christ says, "If anyone takes your coat, let him have your cloak as well" [Matt. 5:40]. But you may say, "If that is the meaning of 'doing God's will,' who, then, can be saved? Who can fulfil this lofty commandment to the extent that he surrenders all things and has no will of his own?" This is my reply: You must learn how important and necessary this petition is, why we must pray it ardently and earnestly, and why it is important that our will be mortified and God's will alone be done. Thus you must confess that you are a sinner who cannot do God's will, who must petition God for help and mercy, to forgive your shortcomings, and to aid you in doing his will. It is imperative that if God's will is to prevail, our will must be submerged, for these two are at war with each other. We can take an example from Christ, our Lord. When he asked his Father in the garden to remove the cup, he also added, "Not my will, but thine, be done" [Luke 22:42]. If Christ had to surrender his will, which after all was good, yes, undoubtedly and always the best, in order that God's will be carried out, why should we poor little worms make such a fuss about our will, which is never free of evil and always deserves to be thwarted?

To understand this we must note the two ways in which our will is evil. In the first place, our will may be openly and patently and undisguisedly evil, as, for example, when we are wilfully inclined to do something that is generally acknowledged by all as being evil; such as a will to be wrathful, to lie, deceive, to harm a neighbor, to be unchaste, and the like. Such a will and leaning show up in everyone, especially when he is incited in their direction. We must ask God's help in opposing it, so that his will may be done, for God wants peace, truth, purity, and gentleness. In the second place, our will may appear cloaked and disguised as something good, as seen for instance in the words in Luke 9 [54-55], directed by St. John and St. James against the Samaritans who would not receive Christ, "Lord, do you want us to bid fire come down from heaven and consume them?" The Lord answered them, "Do you not know what manner of spirit you are children of; for the Son of man came not to destroy the soul but to save it."

To this category belong all who fly in the face of the supposed injustice or folly done them or others. Whatever they undertake must succeed. When thwarted, they lament, "Oh, I meant so very well. Oh, I wanted to help a whole city, but the devil will not have it." They imagine that they are obligated to be vexed and angered and thus to sow discord between themselves and others and to raise the hue and cry that their good will was frustrated. But if they would look at the matter in the light of day they would discover that it was all sham and that they, with their good will, were looking only to their own advantage and honor, their own will and opinion. It is impossible for a truly good and sincere will to become irritable and quarrelsome when thwarted.

Mark well that it is a definite sign of an evil will that it will not brook opposition. Impatience is the fruit by which you can recognize a feigned, false, and cunning good will. A genuinely good will when thwarted will say, "O God, I regarded my plan as good. But if it is not to be, I am content. May your will be done." Wherever there is dissension and impatience, there can be nothing that is good, no matter how good it may seem or want to be.

In addition to these two evil wills, there is a just and good will, which also must not be done. David had such a will when he wanted to build a temple to God. The Lord praised him for this, and yet did not permit him to carry it out.[18] Such was the will of Christ in the garden when he was reluctant to drink the cup; his will, though good, did not prevail. Likewise, if you willed to con-

---

[18] Cf. II Sam. 7:22-29.

vert the whole world, raise the dead, lead yourself and all others to heaven, and to perform every miracle, you should still not want to do any of this unless you had first consulted God's will and subordinated your will wholly to his, and said, "My dear God, this or that seems good to me; if you approve, let it be done, but if you disapprove, let it remain undone."

God very often breaks this good will in his saints to prevent a false, malicious, and evil good will from establishing itself through the semblance of good, and also to help us learn that no matter how good our will may be, it is still immeasurably inferior to God's will. Therefore, our inferior good will must necessarily give way to the infinitely better will of God; it must submit to being destroyed by it.

Third, this good will in us must be hindered for its own improvement. God's only purpose in thwarting our good will is to make of it a better will. And this is done when it subordinates itself to and conforms to the divine will (by which it is hindered), until the point is reached when man is entirely unfettered by his own will, delivered from his own will, and knows nothing except that he waits upon the will of God.

Now that is what is meant by genuine obedience, a thing which, unfortunately, is entirely unknown in our day. Nowadays idle babblers come along and fill all of Christendom with their chatter and mislead the poor people with their doctrines. They fairly shout from the pulpits telling us how to have and how to make a good will, a good opinion, a good resolve. Then they tell the people that if they have done this they can feel secure and that all that they do is good. With this doctrine they merely create self-willed and stubborn people, bold and secure minds, who constantly contend against God's will and do not break or subordinate their own. They feel that their own ideas are good and should therefore prevail, and that whatever obstructs them must be of the devil and not of God. That gives birth to the wolves in sheep's clothing, to those arrogant saints who are the most pernicious people on earth. That is why one bishop fights and feuds and wars with another, one church with another. That is why priests and monks and nuns are at loggerheads with each other. That is why there is dissension everywhere. Yet each faction claims to have a good will, the right opinion, and a godly resolve. And so they carry on their devilish work, thinking it to be to the honor and glory of God.

One ought to teach them properly to have a God-fearing will and not to rely in the least on their own will and opinion, yes, to cast from them this accursed belief that they can have or make a good will or intention. Man must despair utterly of ever having or attaining a good will, opinion, or resolve. As I stated before, a good will is found only where there is no will. Where there is no will, God's will, which is the very best, will be present. Therefore these barkers know all about a good or a bad will. They come along boldly and encourage us to say with our lips, "Thy will be done," but with the heart, "My will be done." Thus they mock God and us.

You may say, "Well, did God not endow us with a free will?"[19] I reply: To be sure, he gave you a free will. But why do you want to make it your own will? Why not let it remain free? If you do with it whatever you will, it is not a free will, but your own will. God did not give you or anyone else a will of your own. Your own will comes from the devil and from Adam, who transformed the free will received from God into his own. A free will does not want its own way, but looks only to God's will for direction. By so doing it then also remains free, untrammeled and unshackled.

Summary

In this petition you will notice that God bids us to pray against ourselves. In that way he teaches us that we have no greater enemy than ourself. You see, our will is the most formidable element in us, and against it we must pray, "O Father, do not let me get to the point where my will is done. Break my will; resist it. No matter what happens let my life be governed not by my will, but by yours. As no one's own will prevails in heaven so may it also be here on earth." Such a petition or its fulfilment is indeed very painful to our human nature, for our own will is the greatest and most deep-rooted evil in us, and nothing is dearer to us than our own will.

Therefore, we are asking for nothing else in this petition than

---

[19] On free will, see *Disputation Against Scholastic Theology* (1517). *LW* 31, 3-16; and the *Heidelberg Disputation* (1518). *LW* 31, 58-70. Cf. also Luther's *The Bondage of the Will (De Servo Arbitrio,* 1525). *WA* 18, (551) 605-787.

the cross, torment, adversity, and sufferings of every kind, since these serve the destruction of our will. If these self-willed people really thought about this and noted that they are praying against their own will, they would turn against this petition or even be frightened by it.

Now let us relate these three petitions to each other. The first asks that God's name be honored and that his glory and honor may dwell in us. But no one can attain to that unless he is righteous and lives in the kingdom of God. The dead and the sinners cannot praise God, as David declares in Psalm 6 [:5]. And no one is godly unless he is free of sin. Only he is free of sin whose own will is uprooted and replaced by God's will alone. For if the will, the chief and head of all our members, is no longer ours and is no longer evil, then all other members are also no longer ours and no longer evil. Consequently, this petition seizes evil by the head, not by the hand or the foot, but by our will, which is the chief of all evil, the true arch-knave.

The Fourth Petition

Give us this day our daily bread

Until now we used the little word "thy." But now we shall speak of "our," "ours," "us," etc. We want to find the reason for this.

When God hears us in the first three petitions and hallows his name in us, he incorporates us into his kingdom and pours into us his grace, which begins to make us godly. As soon as this grace starts to do God's will, it encounters a resisting Adam. Thus St. Paul laments in Romans 7 [:19] that he does not do what he wants very much to do. One's own will, inborn from Adam, contends with all our members against the good impulses. Then the grace in our hearts cries to God for help against this Adam and says, "Thy will be done." For man finds himself heavily burdened with his own self.

When God hears this cry, he resolves to come to the aid of his precious grace and to enlarge his newborn kingdom. He attacks the arch-knave, the old Adam, with might and main, inflicts all kinds of adversity on him, thwarts all of his plans, and blinds him and foils him on every side. This occurs when God visits all kinds of woe and grief upon us. Slanderous tongues and evil, unfaithful men are the means for this. And where such men are not adequate, the devils themselves have to serve this end. All this takes place so that our will shall be throttled with all its evil inclinations and so that God's will may be done in such a way that grace may reign in the kingdom and only God's glory and honor prevail.

When this happens, man finds himself beset by great fear and anxiety and cannot in the least imagine that this experience is related to the doing of God's will. No, he now imagines that he has been abandoned into the hands of the devils and evil men, and that there is no longer a God in heaven who cares to know and hear him. Then the real hunger and thirst of the soul make themselves known as the soul yearns for solace and help. This hunger is far more tormenting than physical hunger. Now the word "our" comes into its own; now we long to satisfy our need, and we say, "Give us this day our daily bread."

But how is that done? God has allotted us much tribulation in this world, and, at the same time, offered us no other consolation than his holy Word. Thus Christ has promised us, "In the world you will have tribulation, but in me you will have peace" [John 16:33]. Therefore, if you are willing to have God's kingdom come to you and have God's will be done, do not resort to evasive measures. It cannot be otherwise: God's will is done only if yours is not done. That is to say, the more adversity you experience, the better is God's will done; this is especially true in the hour of death. It has been ordained—and no one can alter this—that in this world we find unrest, and in Christ we find peace.

In this tribulation the evil people are separated from the good. The evil people, who soon fall from grace and defect from the new kingdom of God, do not understand God's will and do not know the purpose of their tribulation or how to conduct themselves in it. Therefore they return to their own will and expel grace very much as a spoiled stomach does the food which it cannot digest. Some become impatient, and revile, curse, blaspheme, and rave. Others run hither and yon in search of human solace and counsel, hoping to rid themselves of their adversities and to overcome and suppress their adversaries. In brief, they want to be their own saviors and redeemers and are unwilling to wait for God to relieve them of their cross. They all do themselves infinite harm. God had begun to mortify their will, to build the kingdom of his grace in them, to raise up the glory and honor of his name in them, and to establish his will in them. Now they refuse his divine healing hand. They fall back and cling to their own will, that old knave. Yes, like the Jews, they release the criminal Barabbas [Matt. 27:15-23] and kill the innocent Son of God, that is, the grace of God, which had just begun to take root in them. Psalm 106 [:13] says of them, "They would not accept what God had planned to do with them."

The righteous are wise and well aware of the purpose of the divine will, even though it involves all kinds of adversity. They also know what their proper attitude over against this must be. They know that no enemy has ever been put to flight by a fleeing person. By the same token, no suffering or affliction or death can be overcome by impatience, flight, or search for release, but only by persistently standing one's ground and by going forth boldly to face adversity and death. The saying is true: "He who fears hell will plunge into it." Thus he who is afraid of death will be eternally devoured by it. He who shrinks from suffering will suffer defeat. Fear works no good. Therefore we must be brisk and bold in these matters and stand firmly.

But who is able to do that? This petition teaches you where you may seek solace and how you may find peace in such disquietude. You must say, "O Father, give us our daily bread." That is to say, "O Father, with your divine Word comfort me, a poor and miserable wretch. I cannot bear your hand, and yet I know that it works to my damnation if I do not bear it. Therefore, strengthen me, my Father, lest I despair." In his will, that is, in our suffering, God does not want us to run anywhere, to run to anyone but him. We are not to seek release from this suffering, for that would result in our harm and be a hindrance to the divine will and to our welfare. No, we must ask for strength to endure his will. It is true that no one is able to suffer and to die fearlessly (which God, after all, wants us to do) unless he is strengthened for this. There is no creature that can give us this strength. On the contrary, all creatures, especially man, are more apt to make us weak and inconstant and yielding, if we should seek comfort and help from them.

Therefore, it is only the Word of God or our daily bread that must strengthen us. This is what God says through the mouth of Isaiah, "The Lord God has given me a wise tongue so that I may know how to sustain them that are weary" [Isa. 50:4]. And in Matthew 11 [:28] we read, "Come to me, all who labor and are heavy-laden, and I will give you rest." And in Psalm 119 [:28] David says, "Strengthen me with thy word," and in Psalm 130 [:5], "My soul has relied on his word." With such teachings the entire Scriptures are full, full, full!

Now, when and by whom does the Word come to us? It comes in a twofold manner. In the first place, it comes to us by a person; for instance, when God through a pastor in the church or by another lets us hear a comforting and strengthening word, a word that makes us feel in our heart: Take courage, and be strong. That is surely the sound made in our hearts if the Word of God rightly comes to us. Therefore we should strive to keep from sick and dying people womanish prattle and women who say, "Dear relatives and dear Jack, do not worry, for you will soon be well and happy and rich again." Such talk creates faint and weak and soft hearts, although we hear the Word of God described as "bread to strengthen man's heart" [Ps. 104:15]. Therefore I would reply, "Dear friends, eat your rotten porridge yourself; I shall wait for the daily bread which will sustain me." This is how the sick should be emboldened and strengthened for death and the suffering be encouraged to endure more suffering. If they should say that they are unable to do this, remind them of this petition and to implore God for strength, for he wants to be asked for it.

In the second place, this Word comes to us directly as, for instance, when God pours his Word into the heart of a suffering person, imparting strength to endure all. After all, God's Word is all-powerful. But since there are many words of God, which word is meant here? Answer: No one can say that definitely, for the words of God are as diverse as man's ailments and woes. One word must be spoken to the fainthearted, another to the stiffnecked. The latter must be shocked, the former encouraged. Since we are now speaking of people in whom God's will is being done and who are

52

distressed and afflicted, words that will give strength are in order, words such as Paul uses when addressing the Hebrews in chapter 12. But since the proper choice of the words of God, as also their effectiveness, does not rest with men but solely with God, we ought to ask God that he himself might select the holy words for us and that they be given us either directly by him or by another human being.

Now the plain truth is that he who has never been tried by suffering and has never experienced the power of the Word of God to give strength, cannot know the true purport of this petition. Such comfort cannot appeal to him, for he has known and tasted only his own and other creatures' comfort and aid. He has never drunk a cup of woe to the dregs and been disconsolate. Therefore, because this is a profound petition, we will discuss one word after another and search for the full meaning of this petition.

The first word is "our." This word declares that here we are not asking primarily for ordinary bread, which is also eaten by the heathen and given unbidden to all men by God, but are asking for "our bread" because we are children of the heavenly Father. So then, we are addressing a heavenly and spiritual, not an earthly, Father in this petition, and we ask not for earthly, but for heavenly and spiritual bread, which is ours and which we as heavenly children need. Otherwise it would not be necessary to say "our daily bread"; physical bread would be adequately identified by the words, "Give us this day the daily bread." God wishes to teach his children to be more concerned about food for the soul; yes, he even forbids them to worry about their bodily food and drink.

The second word is "daily." The Greek word for "daily" is *epiousion.* This has been interpreted variously. Some say it denotes a spiritual bread; others, a choice and extraordinary bread; others, following the Hebrew language, say it means a bread for tomorrow. It is not synonymous with the German "breakfast" [*Morgenbrot*], used in contrast to "supper" [*Abendbrot*], but it is a bread prepared for the next day, in Latin, *crastinum,* tomorrow. No one needs to be confused by this multiplicity of definitions, for they all reflect but one meaning, namely, the proper expression of the kind and nature of this bread.

In the first place, it specifies a supernatural bread, since God's

Word does not nourish man bodily and naturally in his mortal frame. It nourishes him as an immortal and supernatural being, yes, far beyond his present existence even as an eternal being. Christ says, "He who eats this bread will live for ever" [John 6:51, 58]. Hence this petition means to say, "Father, give us the supernatural, immortal, eternal bread."

In the second place, it is called a select, tender, and dainty bread, most delightful and pleasant to the taste. In the Wisdom of Solomon 16 [:20] we read that this heavenly bread "is suited to every taste." Thus our heavenly bread is much nobler, finer, and more delicious and abounding more in all grace and virtue than natural bread. As a select bread it may also be understood to be a particular and peculiar bread, appropriate to us as children of God and given exclusively to us. It is *egregius, peculiaris, proprius*.[20] Thus the Apostle says to the Hebrews [13:10] that we have a special altar from which no one but we may eat. Thus we have an unusual and particular bread.

In the third place, in Hebrew this is called the bread for tomorrow. The Hebrew language uses the word "tomorrow" when we Germans use the word "daily." In German the term "daily" refers to that which we have on hand ready for use, even though it is not used continuously. We say for instance, "I must have this or that today or tomorrow or daily and I must have it on hand, though I do not know at what hour I may need it." The Hebrew language expresses this very idea with the little word *cras*, "for the morrow," or *crastinum*,[21] "tomorrow." Thus Jacob says to Laban in Genesis [30:33], "My honesty will answer for me later"; that is, my honesty will answer for me and justify me today or tomorrow or whenever it happens to be. The meaning of the prayer is that God may give us the supernatural bread, our select, peculiar, and daily bread— daily so that we have it on hand and are constantly supplied with it against the time of need and suffering (which we may expect daily), so that it might strengthen us, lest we be taken unawares and despair and perish and die eternally from want of it.

We must note here that we Christians ought to be richly and

---

[20] I.e., excellent, particular, peculiar.
[21] Actually, the terms are Latin.

abundantly supplied with this bread. We should be so well versed and instructed in the Word of God that we have it at hand daily in all trials and will be able to strengthen ourselves and others. This is what the dear saints were able to do, as we gather from their epistles and biographies. But we are at fault when we suffer want because we do not ask God for this bread. In consequence, we have ignorant bishops, priests, and monks, who have nothing to give us. And we, in turn, make a bad situation worse by loathing, ridiculing, and despising them. God's wrath brings matters to such a pass! Therefore we should examine this petition closely. In it God teaches us to pray for all spiritual leaders, especially for those who are supposed to offer us the Word of God. It will not be given to them unless we prove ourselves worthy of it and ask God for it. Therefore, when you see untrained and incompetent bishops, priests, or monks, do not curse, condemn, or rebuke them, but regard them as a horrible plague from God by means of which he punishes you and us all for not praying the Lord's Prayer and for not asking him for our daily bread. If we would sincerely pray the Lord's Prayer and ask for our daily bread, God would surely hear us and send us fine, capable, and learned spiritual leaders. We are at fault more than they. Nowadays we find people whom God punishes by so hardening their hearts that they not only fail to recognize our untrained clergy as a plague, but even take delight in despising them and making light of this deserved plague of God, whereas they should really be weeping bloody tears, if this were possible, over such a serious and severe plague inflicted on us by God. I want you to know that God has never yet punished the world more harshly than by allowing blind and ignorant leaders to exist, who destroy us by withholding the Word of God and our bread. Let the Turks be Turks. This plague surpasses them.[22] Woe unto us for not realizing this and praying for it to cease!

On the other hand, God has never been more gracious to the world than when he granted it well-informed and devoted spiritual

---

[22] While not disloyal to his emperor in his battles against the Turks, Luther saw godlessness and the German internal chaotic conditions as evils worse than the Turks. Cf. *On War Against the Turk* (1529). *LW* 46, 155-206; and *Appeal for Prayer Against the Turks* (1541). *LW* 43, 213-242.

leaders, who supplied this Word daily and abundantly. Christendom, and every Christian soul, is born in and through the Word of God. Therefore they must also be nourished, preserved, and protected by it. Without it, they will perish more wretchedly than does the body when deprived of its physical bread.

The third word is "bread." The Scriptures assign many different names to the Word of God because of its many virtues and effects. It is indeed all things and all-powerful [Heb. 1:3; 4:12]. It is called "the sword of the Spirit" [Eph. 6:17], with which we combat the devil and all spiritual foes. It is termed "a light" [Ps. 119:105], "the early and the late rain" [Jas. 5:7], "a heavenly dew" [Hos. 6:4], "gold, silver" [Ps. 119:72], medicine, garment, ornament, and the like. Similarly, it is also called bread, since it nourishes and strengthens the soul, which grows strong and fat on it. The term is not to be understood in its narrow sense. Just as Scripture uses the physical bread to designate all sorts of precious bodily food, so also the spiritual bread encompasses the innumerable kinds of food for the soul. There is a diversity of souls on earth and each has its own need and requirement. Yet the Word of God satisfies the needs of all and of each individually. If the food of all kings who ever lived and who ever will live were gathered in one heap, it could not in the least be compared with the smallest word of God. Therefore Christ in the Gospel likens this to a marriage feast, etc. [Matt. 22:1-10], and Isaiah to a costly, choice, and magnificent banquet [Isa. 25:6].

What is the bread or the Word of God?

The bread, the Word, and the food are none other than Jesus Christ our Lord himself. Thus he declares in John 6 [:51], "I am the living bread which came down from heaven to give life to the world." So then, let no one be deceived by words or false appearances. Sermons and doctrines which do not bring and show Jesus Christ to us are not the daily bread and nourishment of our souls, nor will they help us in any need or trial.

The fourth word is "give." No one can obtain the bread, Jesus Christ, by himself, nor by studying, hearing, asking, searching. If we are truly to know Jesus Christ, then all books fall short, all teachers are too feeble, all reason is too limited. The Father himself must reveal him and present him to us, as Christ states in John 6 [:44], "No one can come to me unless the Father who sent me draws him." He says further, "No one can receive me or know me, unless it is given to him by the Father" [John 6:65]. And also, "Everyone who has heard me through the Father comes to me" [John 6:45]. Therefore he teaches us to ask for the blessed bread and to say, "Give it to us today."

Now Christ our bread is given in a twofold manner. In the first place, outwardly, by persons, for instance, by priests or teachers. And this is also done in two different ways: first, through words; second, through the Sacrament of the Altar. Much could be said on this subject. To put it briefly, God confers a great blessing whenever he permits Christ to be preached and taught. Of course, only Christ should everywhere be preached and this daily bread distributed.

In the sacrament Christ is received. However, this would not happen if Christ were not, at the same time, prepared and distributed through the Word. For the Word brings Christ to the people and acquaints their hearts with him. The sacrament in itself does not transmit this knowledge. Therefore, it is a bad situation that in our time so much stress is laid on saying and having masses said, while unfortunately neglecting the most important part, the one for which the masses were instituted, namely, the proclamation.[23] Thus Christ says and commands, "As oft as you do this, do it in remembrance of me" [I Cor. 11:25]. And even if there is some preaching, the mass may be of Christ but the sermon on Theodoric of Bern[24] or some other story. God punishes us in this way because we do not pray for our daily bread. The venerable sacrament finally becomes not only a vain and empty custom but also an object of contempt. After all, what does it profit us if Christ is present and has prepared bread for us, if this bread is not given to us and we do not delight in it? That is just as if a delicious meal were prepared and no one was there to pass the bread, bring the food, or

---

[23] See Luther's treatment of the purpose of the mass on pp. 173-174.
[24] The allusion is to a heroic figure of German legend who typified the wise and just ruler. Derived from Theodoric the Great, he appears in the Nibelung Cycle as the vanquisher of Hagen.

pour the drink, and all were expected to have their hunger appeased by the odor or the sight of the meal. Therefore we should preach only Christ and relate everything to him. All writings should point to him and proclaim why he came, what he brought us, and how we should believe in him and conduct ourselves toward him, so that the people can comprehend Christ and know him through his Word. Then they will not come away from the mass with empty hearts, knowing neither Christ nor themselves.

In the second place, Christ our bread is given us inwardly when taught by God himself. This is also a necessary part of the outward giving, for without it the outer mode of giving is futile. But if the latter is properly carried out, then the inward way cannot remain merely external. God never permits his Word to go forth without leading to fruit. He himself is present and teaches inwardly that which he gives externally through the priest. In Isaiah 55 [:10-11] he says, "For as the rain waters the earth and makes it fruitful, so shall my word be that goes forth from my mouth; it shall not return to me empty, but it shall accomplish that for which I sent it." This is what creates true Christians, who know Christ and who deeply savor him.

You may ask, "What does it mean to know Christ? Or, what does he bring us?" Answer: You learn to know Christ when you comprehend the words of the Apostle recorded in I Corinthians 1 [:30], "Christ was given to us by God to be our wisdom, righteousness, sanctification, and redemption." You comprehend this fully when you realize that all your wisdom is damnable stupidity, your righteousness damnable unrighteousness, your purity damnable impurity, your redemption miserable damnation; and when you thus discover that before God and all creatures you are actually a fool, a sinner, an unclean and condemned man, and when you show not only with words but also with all your heart and your deeds that you are left with no other comfort and salvation than the fact that Christ is given you by God and that you believe in him and partake of him, whose righteousness alone can preserve you, as you appeal to it and rely on it. Such a faith is nothing else than the eating of this bread, as Christ says in John 6 [:32], "My Father gives you the true bread from heaven."

You will say, "Who is so ignorant as not to know that we are sinners, that we are nothing, that we are saved solely by Christ?" Answer: To know and to say this in so many words, or also to hear this, is of course in itself a token of great grace. However, there are but few who comprehend this and can say it with their hearts, and this is borne out by experience. When we scorn people as fools and sinners, they resent it and quickly discover a wisdom and a righteousness of their own, one apart from that of Christ. They forget that Christ is their righteousness, especially when their conscience smites them, both during their lifetime and in the hour of death. Then they frantically search here and there for a way to comfort and bolster their conscience with their good works. And when this does not help (and it certainly cannot help), they despair.[25]

Much could be said about this, and every sermon should deal with it. When Christ is proclaimed and the precious bread is distributed in this way, the souls of men will lay hold of it and apply it in the sufferings which the divine will assigns to them. In that way men's souls become strong and full of faith, no longer fearing their sin or conscience, devil or death. Now you see what is meant by this daily bread and that Christ is truly this bread. However, he will be of no benefit to you and you will not be able to avail yourself of him unless God translates him into words whereby you can hear and know him. What does it profit you if Christ sits in heaven or is hidden in the form of bread? He must be brought to you, prepared for you, and translated into words for you by means of the inner and external word. See, that is truly the Word of God. Christ is the bread, God's Word is the bread, and yet there is but one object, one bread. He is in the Word, and the Word is in him. To believe in this same Word is the same as eating the bread. He to whom God imparts this will live eternally.

The fifth word is "us." Here every person is admonished to embrace all of Christendom in his heart and to pray for himself and for all men, especially for the members of the clergy whose duty it is to administer the Word of God. Just as in the first three petitions we pray that the things which are God's may be granted to us, so we now pray for all of Christendom. There is nothing more

---

[25] See A Sermon on Preparing to Die (1519), in this volume, pp. 99-115.

necessary and profitable for Christendom than this daily bread, that is, that God may grant a well-trained clergy who will preach and make his Word heard throughout the whole world. If the priesthood and the Word of God are true to their purpose, then Christendom will prosper and flourish. He also commanded us to pray for this when he said, "Pray therefore the Lord of the harvest to send out laborers into his harvest" [Matt. 9:38].

So then, true love will prompt us to pray above all else for Christendom, and this accomplishes more than praying just for ourselves. For, as Chrysostom says, all of Christendom prays for him who prays for it.[26] Indeed, in such a prayer he prays together with Christendom for himself. A prayer spoken only in behalf of oneself is not a good prayer. I hope to God that I am not wrong when I feel but little love for some of the brotherhoods,[27] especially those that are so busy with themselves and act as though they alone were going to heaven and would have us remain behind. I ask you to note and to ponder that it is not without reason that Christ taught us to pray "our Father" and not "my Father," "give us this day our daily bread" and not "my daily bread," that he speaks of "our trespasses," "us," and "our." He wants to hear the throngs and not me or you alone, or a single isolated Pharisee. Therefore sing with the congregation and you will sing well. Even if your singing is not melodious, it will be swallowed up by the crowd. But if you sing alone you will have your critics.

The sixth word is "this day." As I said earlier, this term teaches us that God's Word is not in our power. Therefore we must rid ourselves of all false reliance on knowledge, reason, skill, and wisdom. In the hour of trial God himself must cheer, comfort, and sustain us with his Word. Even if the Scriptures abound in passages

---

[26] One of the four great doctors of the Eastern church and patriarch of Constantinople (347-407), Chrysostom was renowned as an eloquent preacher. Cyprian speaks in a similar vein in *On the Lord's Prayer*, 8; it may have been his and not Chrysostom's statement which Luther had in mind.

[27] The brotherhoods, groups of lay men and women attached to existing mendicant orders, were especially popular in the fifteenth century. For their prayers and alms they had a share in the indulgences and good works of the friars. Luther rebuked them and directed them to the "true confraternity of Christ's church." See *The Blessed Sacrament of the True and Holy Body of Christ, and the Brotherhoods* (1519). LW 35, 45-73.

enabling us to teach the whole Word as long as all is tranquil, this will not help us when storms rage, unless God himself appears and speaks either directly to our hearts or through another person. Unless that is done, all is soon forgotten and our ship will sink. Thus we read in Psalm 107 [:27], "They reeled and staggered like drunken men, and were at their wits' end." Then all their wisdom vanishes and they remember nothing at all.

Since we, therefore, live here amidst perils and always in expectation of all kinds of suffering, such as the agony of death and the pain of hell, fear will prompt us to pray that God may not long delay his Word, but may be with us today, now, daily, to give us our daily bread, and, as St. Paul says to the Ephesians [3:16-17], grant that "Christ may appear in us and dwell in our inner man." Therefore we do not say "tomorrow" or "the day after tomorrow," as if today we were secure and delivered from fear. No, we pray "today." It is also better to say "today" than "tomorrow" when God's will is about to be done and our own will dies in agony. Yes, at such a time the word "today" is almost inadequate, and we would wish that the bread be given us in this very hour and not merely today. In the Scriptures the word "today" is also used in the sense of a whole lifetime on earth. However, I shall not enter into that now.

Summary of this petition

This petition means to say, "O heavenly Father, since no one likes your will and since we are too weak to have our will and our old Adam mortified, we pray that you will feed us, strengthen and comfort us with your holy Word, and grant us your grace that the heavenly bread, Jesus Christ, may be preached and heard in all the world, that we may know it in our hearts, and so that all harmful, heretical, erroneous, and human doctrine may cease and only your Word, which is truly our living bread, be distributed.

But do we not also pray for our physical bread?[28] Answer: Yes, this too may well be included in this petition. However, this petition refers principally to Christ, the spiritual bread of the soul.

---

[28] Cf. Luther's expanded interpretation of the physical bread in his catechisms. *The Small Catechism* (1529) and *The Large Catechism* (1529), T. G. Tappert (ed.), *The Book of Concord* (Philadelphia: Fortress Press, 1959), pp. 347, 430-432. Cf. also *LW* 43, 196-197.

This is why Christ teaches us not to worry about our body's food and raiment, but to take thought only for the needs of each day. In Matthew 6 [:34] he says, "Be content with your worry about today. Do not worry about tomorrow, for tomorrow will bring its own worries." It is indeed a good exercise in faith to ask God only for today's bread so that we may then trust in a greater God. This does not mean that we should not work for our daily needs or food, but that we should not worry that we might starve unless we fear and fret. Our toil must be motivated more by our desire to serve God through it, to avoid idleness, and to fulfil God's command addressed to Adam, "In the sweat of your face you shall eat bread" [Gen. 3:19], rather than by our worrying and fretting over our nourishment. God will surely take care of this as long as we do our work according to his commandments.

The Fifth Petition

And forgive us our trespasses, as we forgive
those who trespass against us

Who would believe that this petition would affect and accuse so many people? In the first place, why should the great saints of our day pray it? After all, they consider themselves wholly righteous after they have confessed, been absolved, and have rendered satisfaction; they now live as if it were no longer necessary to pray for forgiveness of their sins, as do the old genuine saints of whom David says, "Every saint will ask for pardon for his sins. Therefore let everyone who is godly offer prayer for them" [Ps. 32:6]. Instead, they amass great merits and with their good works construct a magnificent palace in heaven very close to St. Peter.[29] However, God willing, we will make sinners of them and add them to our poor, sinful kinfolk so that they might learn to pray this petition with us, not only before their confession and penance, but also after their plenary indulgence of penalty and guilt, so that they might join us, even after the absolution and remission of all their

---

[29] Luther alludes to the construction of St. Peter's Church in Rome, which was financed by the sale of indulgences.

sins, and say, "Lord, forgive us our trespasses." Since we cannot lie to God or trifle with him, there must actually be a sin of ours so very grave that no indulgence will or can remit it. Therefore indulgence is not the same thing as this prayer. If all your sin is wiped out by indulgences, then strike out this petition and do not ask God to remit sins that do not exist, lest you mock him and call every adversity down upon your head.

On the other hand, if this petition is valid, then may God have pity on that poor indulgence which leaves such a large residue of guilt, for the sake of which God deservedly damns man if he does not seek his mercy. I am not exaggerating, for I am well acquainted with those subtle glossaries whereby one is wont to make a wax nose out of Holy Scripture.[30]

This petition can be interpreted in two ways. First, it may signify that God forgives us our trespasses secretly when we are unaware of it, even as he reckons and retains many men's sins which they neither feel nor heed. Second, it may mean that God remits them openly so that we are aware of it, even as he at times reckons the sin of some against them so that they are aware of it, for instance, through some penalty or a terrified conscience. The first type of forgiveness is always necessary; the second is occasionally necessary so that man may not despair.

What does this mean?

I say this: God is well-disposed toward many people, forgiving with all his heart all their trespasses, yet without telling them of this. Instead, this inner and external treatment of them leads them to believe that they have a very ungracious God who is determined to condemn them here in time and also in eternity. Outwardly he torments them, inwardly he terrifies them. One of these was David, when he exclaimed in Psalm 6 [:1], "O Lord, do not chasten me in thy wrath." On the other hand, God secretly retains the sins of others and is really angry with them, but keeps them in ignorance of this. He treats them in such a way that they believe that they are his dear children. Outwardly they are well off, inwardly they are happy and sure of heaven. These are described in Psalm

---

[30] I.e., make Scripture say whatever one wishes it to say.

10 [:6], "I shall not be moved; throughout all generations I shall not know adversity." Thus God occasionally allows comfort to come to the conscience and fills man with cheerful confidence in his mercy to strengthen and inspire him with hope in God even in times when his conscience is fearful. On the other hand, God at times saddens and terrifies a conscience so that even in happy days a man will not forget the fear of God.

The first mode of forgiveness is bitter and hard for us, but it is the one most sublime and precious. The second is easier for us, but not as good. Christ shows us both types in Mary Magdalene— the first when he turns his back on her and remarks to Simon that her many sins are forgiven her [Luke 7:47]. In that moment she does not yet feel the peace of conscience. He shows the second type when he turns to her and says that her sins are remitted and that she should go in peace [Luke 7:50]. Now she is at peace. The first renders a person pure; the second confers peace. The first effects and conveys, the second rests and receives. There is a vast difference between the two. The first is only believed and deserves much; the second is felt and gathers in the reward. The first is applied to the strong in faith, the other to the weak, to the beginners in the faith.[31]

We now take a look at the mightiest letter of indulgence that ever came to earth, one which, moreover, cannot be bought with money but is given free to everyone. Other teachers drop our remission into our purse or money-chest;[32] Christ places it into our hearts. It cannot be brought closer to us than that, and now you need not hasten to Rome, or to Jerusalem, or to St. James;[33] you need not run hither and yon in quest of indulgence. Now the poor can obtain this as well as the rich, the sick as well as the healthy, the layman as well as the priest, the servant as well as the master. This letter of indulgence reads, "If you forgive them their trespasses,

---

[31] The next section was also printed as a separate article. Dated 1523, it appeared under the title *Christ, the Letter of Indulgence (Christus Ablassbrief)* in a larger work that dealt with the position of Luther and Melanchthon toward Erasmus and included a statement by Luther concerning the degree to which the preaching of the gospel requires the elements of severity and mercy.

[32] I.e., in return for money, an indulgence letter is given.

[33] I.e., places of pilgrimage. Cf. p. 40, n. 16.

your heavenly Father also will forgive you; but if you do not forgive men their trespasses, neither will your Father forgive your trespasses" [Matt. 6:14-15]. This letter, sealed with Christ's own wounds and confirmed by his death, was almost effaced and blotted out by the mighty cloudburst of Roman indulgences!

No one can now excuse himself by saying that his sins are not forgiven or that he must have a bad conscience. For Christ does not say, "Because of your sins you must fast this much or pray this much or donate this much or do this or that." Rather does he say, "If you would render satisfaction and atone for your guilt and wipe out your sins, listen to my advice, yes, to my command, 'The only thing for you to do is to forgive and to renew your heart.' No one can hinder you in this. Be kind to the person who has offended you. As long as you forgive, all will be well."

Why is it that no one preaches about such an indulgence? Are the words, the counsel, and the promise of Christ less valid than the pronouncements of a visionary preacher? Of course, such an indulgence will erect not St. Peter's Church (which the devil likes),[34] but Christ's church (which the devil does not like at all). Christ is not disturbed very much by wood and stone, but by pious and peaceful hearts, which cause him much woe at heart. This indulgence[35] does not have very strong appeal, though it is without cost; whereas people never become sated with the other despite its high cost. It is not that I condemn Roman indulgence.[36] I simply want to see that everything is assigned its proper value. When genuine gold can be had free, it is a mistake to place a higher value on copper. Do not be mislead by the color and the sheen![37]

There are two classes of people who cannot pray this petition and who cannot obtain this great indulgence. The first cannot obtain it for a very obvious reason. They are blind to their own sin and so magnify that of their neighbor that they can declare impudently, "I will not and cannot forgive him. I will never be reconciled to him." They have a beam, indeed many beams, in their own eye,

---

[34] Cf. p. 62, n. 29.
[35] I.e., Christ's indulgence.
[36] On the issue of indulgences, see *LW* 31, xv-xxi; 19-22; see also *Explanations of the Ninety-five Theses* (1518). *LW* 31, 175-185.
[37] The separate article noted on p. 64, n. 31, ends at this point.

but they fail to see them. However, they cannot overlook the smallest stick in their neighbor's eye [Matt. 7:3-5]. That is to say, they pay little heed to the sins they commit against God, but the sin of their neighbor weighs very heavy in their balances. Yet they expect God to forgive their great guilt, while they refuse to let the lesser sins go unavenged. Even in the absence of any other sin or guilt, this beam in their eye would loom very large, namely, their disobedience to God's commandment in refusing to forgive and in insisting on exercising (God's exclusive right of) vengeance. And it is indeed a wondrous God whose justice and judgment stipulate that he who refuses to forgive another is more guilty than he who has committed the wrong and inflicted the harm.

For such people this petition becomes a sin, as we read in Psalm 109 [:7], "Let his prayer be counted as sin before God." By this petition man condemns himself. He completely reverses this prayer so that instead of obtaining mercy he incurs God's displeasure. When you declare that you will not forgive and yet stand before God with your precious Lord's Prayer and your lips babble, "Forgive us our trespasses, as we forgive those who trespass against us," is this not the same as saying, "O God, as I am your debtor, so I also have a debtor; since I will not forgive him, do not forgive me. I will not obey you, even though you bid me to forgive my neighbor. I would rather do without you, your heaven, and all else and go to the devil eternally"?

You wretch, see whether you have an enemy or whether you would endure an enemy who damns you before men as fully as you damn yourself before God and all the saints with your very own prayer. And what harm has such a person done you? Simply a temporal harm. Why would you, because of this trivial, temporal hurt, bring eternal harm to yourself? Beware O man! Not he who offends you but you who refuses to forgive inflicts a harm on you greater than the whole world could do.

The others are more subtle. They are those who are offended spiritually by their neighbor. The thing that disturbs them in others is that these do not appeal to them because of their great love (as they imagine it to be) for righteousness and wisdom. These sensitive and tender saints cannot stand sin and folly. In the Scriptures they are called serpents and venomous vermin [Matt. 23:33]. They are so stark blind that they cannot see nor can they be persuaded (as the previous group of coarse sinners can) that they are the ones who do not forgive their neighbor, yes, that they regard their hostile attitude toward their neighbor as a meritorious work. They are recognized by the fact that they talk about, judge, and condemn everything their neighbor does and never conceal anything they know about him. In German these people are called backbiters, in Greek "devils," in Latin "slanderers," in Hebrew "Satan." In brief, they are composed of that accursed rabble that casts suspicion on everybody and scorns and condemns all, but always under the guise of holiness. This satanic, hellish, and accursed plague unfortunately rages in Christendom more devastatingly today than any other pestilence ever did. It poisons almost every tongue, and—may God have mercy!—people neither heed nor worry about this pitiful condition. They are the people who show him who makes a misstep no mercy, do not (as befits Christians) pray for him, instruct him kindly, or chasten him in a brotherly fashion. According to the divine and human law, a transgressor is faced with but one judge, one court, and one accusation, but these hellish and venomous tongues force us to face as many judges, courts, and accusations as there are ears that hear of our misdeeds, even though these number a thousand daily. These are the miserable saints who do not come to forgive or forget their neighbor's sin. It is in their nature never to be well disposed in their heart toward any person. Thus they not only never become worthy of God's forgiveness, but God's displeasure with them will not even let them recognize their sin.

They then preen and say, "Indeed, I am not saying this to injure my neighbor, nor with any evil intent. I wish him everything good." See what soft fur the little kitten has! Who would imagine that such sharp claws and tongues were concealed under this smooth cover! O you hypocrite and charlatan! If you really were your neighbor's friend you would keep silent and not spread his misfortune with such delight and relish. Your accursed displeasure would change into pity and compassion. You would excuse him, cover up his wrongdoing, bid others to be silent, pray to God on his behalf, admonish him as a brother, and help him to rise again.

Finally, you would also let this be a reminder and a warning to you to ponder your own frailty with a fearful heart, as St. Paul says, "Therefore let anyone who thinks that he stands take heed lest he fall" [I Cor. 10:12]. Then you would say with the holy patriarch: Yesterday it was he; today it is my turn.

Also ponder whether you would like to have God deal with you as you deal with your neighbor, in agreement with this petition. How would you like it if God would retain your sins and spread them abroad into all the world? Or how would you take it if another were to broadcast all your evils? Without a doubt you want everyone to keep quiet about them, forgive them, cover them up, and pray for you. As it is, you are flying in the face of nature and its law which says,"Whatever you wish that men would do to you, do so to them" [Matt. 7:12].

Do not ever suppose that either the slightest or the gravest sins of a backbiter, slanderer, and malicious judge are forgiven until he performs the one good work of bridling and changing his evil tongue. For St. James says, "If anyone thinks he is religious, and does not bridle his tongue but deceives his heart, this man's religion is vain" [Jas. 1:26].

However, if you really do want to do something about your neighbor's sin, then observe the noble and precious golden rule of Christ when he says, "If your brother sins against you, go and tell him his fault, between you and him alone" [Matt. 18:15]. Note that you are not to tell other people about it, but to keep it between him and you alone. Christ says as it were: If you do not want to speak to him alone about it, then hold your tongue and bury it in your heart. As Ecclesiasticus [19:10] says, "It will not make your stomach burst."

Oh, if a person would only busy himself with this noble work, how easily he could atone for his sins, even in the absence of much else! Even if he sins again, God will say, "This man has covered up and forgiven his neighbor's guilt. Gather around, all you creatures, and in turn cover up his sin." He shall never be reproached for his sin.

But nowadays people have recourse to many different ways and modes of rendering satisfaction and doing penance for their sins. They neither see nor hear our daily prayer which reveals that the best way to atone for sin, to render satisfaction, and to obtain forgiveness is to forgive those who trespass against us. The mighty pomp of indulgences and the fear inspired by the precepts of confession cause us to forget and to disregard this. Instead, these people come along and paint the devil over their neighbor's door, whitewash themselves, and say, "Well, is this not true? Why should I not say it if it is true? I saw it and know this is so." Answer: It is equally true that you have sinned. Why do you not, then, speak of your own faults, since you have a mandate to speak the whole truth? However, if you wish to keep your own sins secret, then obey the natural law and do the same for others. Furthermore, even if you are telling the truth, you are no better than traitors and those who betray their own kind, for they also say things that are completely true about many a poor man.

Furthermore, you are violating Christ's precept which forbids you to speak to anyone about your neighbor's fault but to him alone. An exception is made if he refuses to listen to you. Then you are to take one or two persons along with you and repeat your story. If he still refuses to heed you, you, together with the witnesses, are to cite him before the entire congregation [Matt. 18:15-17]. However, this rule has fallen into disuse today. That is why those who ignore God's Word fare as they do.

This widespread vice of backbiting and judging the sins of others is just about the most accursed sin on earth. All other sins contaminate and harm only him who commits them, but this miserable yelping cur has to befoul and ruin himself with the sins of others. And take note of this: the greater one's delight in sin, the greater the sin. But when a sinner reproaches himself for his own sin, when he is ashamed of it and chastens himself, when he hopes that it be kept secret, and thus greatly lessens his guilt, this yelping cur comes along, falls into the same mire like a sow, wallows in it and even devours it, and rejoices that the sin has been committed for he enjoys speaking about it, judging it, and laughing about it. Therefore, as I said before, he who is fond of yelping and backbiting is no man's friend; in fact, he is a common enemy of mankind, just like the devil. This yelper's greatest delight is to hear, to speak about, and to dwell upon his neighbor's sin and shame and to gloat over his evils. And he who enjoys and loves this can surely wish man not what is good, but only misfortune. In the end this will turn out to be his own reward.

Thus we are admonished to learn not only that we are sinners against God, but that there are those who sin and trespass against us.

In the first place, we are gross and vile sinners. There are very few who have not committed great and grave sins. But even if a person is so pious as not to have fallen into such grave sins, he still constantly falls short of satisfying God's commandments. Having received a greater measure of grace than others, he can never repay and thank God adequately even for his most insignificant gifts. Indeed, he is unable to praise God sufficiently for his every-day coat or cloak, to say nothing of life, health, honor, possessions, friends, intellect, and innumerable other blessings from God. Consequently, if God were to call him to account, he could not, as the holy Job says, "answer him once in a thousand times" [Job 9:3], and would be happy to ask only for a merciful judge. Thus David says, "Enter not into judgment with thy servant; for no man living is righteous before thee" [Ps. 143:2]. The fact that no one is so pious as not to have in himself some odor and leaven of the old Adam is enough reason for God justly to reject man. Humility alone, therefore, will preserve even those who live in grace. Their sins will not be imputed to them if they denounce their sins, ask for mercy, and forgive their debtors.

In the second place, we too have debtors. God orders matters so that someone will damage our property, impair our honor, or work some other harm. Thereby he affords us an opportunity to atone for our sin and to forgive our debtors. And even if we do not suffer great wrongs at the hands of others (which, after all, is not a good sign), we will at least find that we harbor a dislike for someone whom we may not trust or with whom we are annoyed. Thus, in brief, St. Augustine's statement is true indeed that every man is a debtor to God and, in turn, has a debtor.[38] If he does not realize this, he is surely blind and does not see himself properly.

---

[38] The theology of Augustine (354-430) had a profound influence on Luther. See Augustine's *Enchiridion,* 73.

Now see how wretched this life is, being devoid of food and comfort and nourishment for the soul, as the preceding petition demonstrates. Furthermore, it is a sinful estate in which we would deservedly be damned if this petition did not uphold us by God's pure mercy and compassion. Thus the Lord's Prayer makes us see this life as being so full of sin and shame that we become weary and tired of it. And now, you yelping cur, judge yourself, speak about yourself, see what you are, search your own heart, and you will soon forget the faults of your neighbor. You will have both hands full with your own faults, yes, more than full!

The Sixth Petition

And lead us not into temptation or trials

If the word "temptation" [39] were not in such general use, it might add to the clarity of this petition to say, And lead us not into trials. This petition brings to our attention the miserable life that we lead here on earth. It is nothing more than one great trial. He who seeks peace and security here acts unwisely, for he will never find them. Though we all strive for them, it is still futile. This is and will ever remain a life of trials.

Therefore we do not say, "Spare us the trial," but, "Do not lead us into it." It is as if we were to say, "We are surrounded on all sides by trials and cannot avoid them; however, dear Father, help us so that we do not fall prey to them and yield to them, and thus be overcome and vanquished." He who gives way to them sins and becomes captive to sin, as St. Paul declares [Rom. 7:23].

Thus, as Job asserts, this life is nothing but combat and struggle against sin. That dragon the devil assails us constantly, bent on swallowing us with his jaws, prompting St. Peter to say, "O dear brethren, be sober, be watchful. Your adversary the devil prowls around like a roaring lion, seeking someone to devour" [I Pet. 5:8]. Now our dear father and faithful bishop St. Peter tells us here that our enemy lies in wait for us, not only in one place but everywhere. In other words, he says that all our members and senses hinder us,

---

[39] Luther uses the word *Anfechtung*. On this term, see p. 181.

lure us on, and move us to unchastity, anger, pride, greed, and the like, inwardly by evil thoughts, outwardly with unchaste pictures, words, and deeds, by men and all creatures. He uses every wile and cunning to beguile man into yielding. As soon as we notice this, we must quickly lift our eyes to God and pray, "O my God and Father, see how I am being tempted and lured into this or that vice and how I am hindered in doing this or that good work. Defend and help me, dear Father; do not let me succumb and be ensnared." O how blessed is he who properly repeats this petition! There are many who are not aware that they are being tempted or who are at a loss to know what to do when temptations come.

What is meant by the word "trials"? There are two kinds of trials. The one comes on the left side. That is the trial which incites us to anger, hatred, embitterment, aversion, and impatience and includes sickness, poverty, dishonor, and all that distresses us, especially when our will, plan, opinion, counsel, words, and deeds are rejected and ridiculed. These are common and daily occurrences in this life and are imposed by God through evil men or devils. When we experience these things we must act wisely and not be surprised, for they are natural to this life. Then we must draw upon prayer and count our true beads,[40] saying, "O Father, this is surely a trial ordained for me. Help me lest it entice and assail me."

In such a trial a man can play the fool in two different ways. In the first place, he plays the fool when he says, "Yes, I will indeed be pious and refrain from anger as long as I am left in peace." There are some people who do not give our God and his saints any rest till he delivers them from the trial. God is then supposed to heal the leg of the one, make another rich, and help a third in his legal affairs. He is supposed to do what they want even if he has to extricate them from their trials at the expense of others. In that way they remain lazy, they remain in fact runaway knights who want neither to be attacked nor to enter combat. This is why they will not be crowned. They indeed fall into the second trial, the one on the right hand, as we shall hear. But where all is as it should be, trials will not pass us by, and we do not seek to avoid them, but

---

[40] An allusion to the prayer beads of the rosary.

to overcome them like a true knight. Of such Job says, "Man's life is a struggle or a trial" [Job 7:1].

The others who do not overcome this trial and also are not relieved of it go their way in anger, hatred, and impatience. They commit themselves wholly to the devil with word and deed, become murderers, blasphemers, profaners, and backbiters, and cause trouble everywhere. The trial has defeated them, and now they yield to every base impulse. The devil has complete power over them, they are his captives, and they call upon neither God nor his saints. But since God himself has called our life a trial, and since it is inevitable that we are assailed in our body, our goods, and our honor, and since injustice is bound to face us, we must view this kindly and accept it wisely, saying, "Well, this is a part of life. What am I to do about it? It is a trial and remains a trial. It is unavoidable. May God aid me so that it does not alarm me or bring me to fall."

So you see that no one is free from trials. However, we can defend ourselves against them and check them by entreating God's help in prayer. Thus we read in the book of hermits[41] how a young brother longed to rid himself of his thoughts. The aged hermit said to him, "Dear brother, you cannot prevent the birds from flying over your head, but you can certainly keep them from building a nest in your hair." Thus, as St. Augustine declares, we cannot prevent trials and temptations from overtaking us, but with our prayer and our invocation of God's assistance we can stave off their victory over us.

The other trial is found on the right hand. It is the trial that lures us to unchastity, lust, pride, greed, and vainglory, to all that appeals to our human nature. It is especially strong when people let us have our way, praise our words, our counsel, and our deeds, and when they honor and esteem us. This is the most pernicious trial. It is assigned to the days of the Antichrist,[42] as David says in Psalm 91 [:7], "A thousand may fall at your left side, then ten thousand at your right hand." It has gained the upper hand today, for the world strives only after wealth, honor, and pleasure. It is

---

[41] I.e., Jerome's *Lives of the Hermits.*
[42] On the Antichrist, see *LW* 44, 133, n. 30.

particularly the youth who no longer learn to contend against carnal lust and temptation. They are so corrupt that they no longer know any shame. The whole world is filled with stories and songs about wenching and harlotry, as though that were perfectly right. This all is a sign of the terrible wrath of God, who permits the world to fall into temptation because no one implores him for help.

A young person is indeed very severely tempted when the devil stirs up his flesh, enflames his marrow and all his members and bones, and when he entices him outwardly with a face, with gestures, dances, dresses, words, and alluring pictures of women or men. As Job says, "His breath kindles coals" [Job 41:21]. At present the world has gone mad with its seductive dress and finery. However, it is not impossible to overcome this temptation if we but cultivate the habit of calling upon God and praying this petition, "Father, do not lead us into this trial." This must also be done when we are tempted by pride, when we are praised and honored, when great wealth or some earthly happiness comes to us, etc.

But why does God let man be thus assailed by sin? Answer: So that man may learn to know himself and God; to know himself is to learn that all he is capable of is sinning and doing evil; to know God is to learn that God's grace is stronger than all creatures. Thus he learns to despise himself and to laud and praise God's mercy. There have been people who tried to resist unchastity with their own strength, with fasting and with work, but they accomplish nothing, though they have deceived their own bodies. Evil passions are extinguished only by the heavenly dew and rain of divine grace. Fasting, work, and vigils are necessary, but in themselves are not sufficient.

Summary

After God has forgiven us our trespasses nothing is so important as being on guard against a relapse. As David says, the big sea of this world teems with vermin, that is, with many trials and temptations, which would have us sin anew.[43] We must therefore sincerely and unceasingly say, "Father, lead me not into trials. I do not ask to be relieved of all trials (for that would be dreadful,

---

[43] Cf. Ps. 104:25.

far worse than ten trials, worse than the trial on the right side), but I do entreat you not to let me fall and sin against my neighbor or against you." Thus St. James says, "My brethren, if many trials assail you, you must rejoice because of it" [Jas. 1:12]. Why? Because trials keep a man alert, perfect him in humility and patience, and make him acceptable to God as his dearest child. Blessed are they who take this to heart, for unfortunately, everyone today seeks tranquillity and peace, pleasure and comfort, in his life. Therefore the rule of the Antichrist is coming closer, if it is not already here.

The Seventh and Last Petition

But deliver us from evil. Amen

Now note that deliverance from evil is the very last thing that we do and ought to pray for. Under this heading we count strife, famine, war, pestilence, plagues, even hell and purgatory, in short, everything that is painful to body and soul. Though we ask for release from all of this, it should be done in a proper manner and at the very last.

Why? There are some, perhaps many, who honor and implore God and his saints solely for the sake of deliverance from evil. They have no other interest and do not ever think of the first petitions which stress God's honor, his name, and his will. Instead, they seek their own will and completely reverse the order of this prayer. They begin at the end and never get to the first petitions. They are set on being rid of their evil, whether this redounds to God's honor or not, whether it conforms to his will or not.

An upright man, however, says, "Dear Father, evil and pain oppress me. I suffer much distress and discomfort. I am afraid of hell. Deliver me from these, but only if this is to your honor and glory and if it agrees with your divine will. If not, then your will, and not mine, be done [Luke 22:42]. Your divine honor and will are dearer to me than my own ease and comfort, both now and eternally." Now that is a pleasing and good prayer and is certain to be heard in heaven. If it is prayed and construed differently, it is displeasing and will not be heard.

75

Since, then, this life is nothing but one accursed evil, in which trials are sure to emerge, we should pray for deliverance from evil so that trials and sin may cease and that God's will may be done and his kingdom come, all to the glory and honor of his holy name.

The Little Word "Amen"

The little word "Amen" is of Hebrew or Jewish origin.[44] In German it means that something is most certainly true. It is good to remember that this word expresses the faith that we should have in praying every petition. Christ says, "Whatever you ask in prayer, you will receive, if you have faith" [Matt. 21:22]. And in another passage he says, "Therefore I tell you, whatever you ask in prayer, believe that you will receive it, and you will" [Mark 11:24]. This is why the Gentile woman was heard: she asked with such persistence and believed so firmly that the Lord said to her, "O woman, great is your faith! Be it done for you as you desire and pray" [Matt. 15:28]. And in James 1 [:6-8] we read, "Let him ask in faith, without doubting, for he who doubts in his faith must not suppose that he will receive anything from the Lord." Therefore the wise man declares that the end of a prayer is better than its beginning [Eccles. 7:8]. If we conclude our prayer with the word "Amen," spoken with confidence and strong faith, it is surely sealed and heard. But without this conclusion neither the beginning nor the middle of the prayer serves any purpose.

So then, before a person begins to pray, he should examine and probe himself to ascertain whether he believes or doubts that his prayer will be fulfilled. If he finds that he doubts or is uncertain, or that he prays at random, the prayer is nothing. His heart is not constant; it wavers and wobbles back and forth, and it is impossible for God to put anything into such a heart, even as you cannot drop anything into a person's hand if he does not hold it still.

Just imagine how you would like it if a person were to entreat

---

[44] Derived from the Hebrew, in which it expressed strong affirmation, this word was accepted by Christians in the Greek New Testament. Luther restored it to use by the congregation for the expression of a firm and hearty faith.

you earnestly and then conclude by saying, "But I do not believe that you will give it to me," although you would surely have given it to him! You would regard his petition as mockery and would retract your promise, and perhaps even punish him. How, then, can we expect it to please God, who promises to grant our petition, when our doubt gives him the lie, when in our prayer we act contrary to the prayer, when we insult his truthfulness, which we invoke in our prayer?

Therefore the little word "Amen" means the same as truly, verily, certainly. It is a word uttered by the firm faith of the heart. It is as though you were to say, "O my God and Father, I have no doubt that you will grant the things for which I petitioned, not because of my prayer, but because of your command to me to request them and because of your promise to hear me. I am convinced, O God, that you are truthful, that you cannot lie. It is not the worthiness of my prayer, but the certainty of your truthfulness, that leads me to believe this firmly. I have no doubt that my petition will become and be an Amen.

In this respect some fail disastrously in their prayer. They nullify it, for they utter it merely with their lips and not with their hearts, because they will not believe that they are heard until they know, or imagine that they know, that they have prayed well and worthily. Thus they build on themselves. They will all be condemned. Such a prayer cannot possibly be sufficient in itself and worthy to be heard by God. No, it must rely on the truthfulness and the promise of God, for if God had not bidden us to pray and promised to hear us, then all creatures could not obtain so much as a kernel of grain with all their prayers. Therefore, take note that a prayer is not good and right because of its length, devoutness, sweetness, or its plea for temporal or eternal goods. Only that prayer is acceptable which breathes a firm confidence and trust that it will be heard (no matter how small and unworthy it may be in itself) because of the reliable pledge and promise of God. Not your zeal but God's Word and promise render your prayer good. This faith, based on God's words, is also the true worship; without it all other worship is sheer deception and error.

A Brief Summary and Arrangement of All the Preceding Petitions[45]

THE SOUL: O our Father, who art in heaven, we your children dwell here on earth in misery, far removed from you. Such a great gulf lies between you and us. How are we to find our way home to you in our fatherland?

GOD, in Malachi 1 [:6]: A child honors its father, and a servant his master. If then I am your Father, where is my honor? If I am your Lord, where is the awe and the reverence due me? For my holy name is blasphemed and dishonored among you and by you, Isaiah 52 [:5].

The First Petition

THE SOUL: My Father, unfortunately that is true. We acknowledge our guilt. Be a merciful Father and do not take us to task, but grant us your grace that your name may be hallowed in us. Let us not think, say, do, have, or undertake anything unless it redounds to your honor and glory. Grant that we may enhance your name and honor above everything else and that we not seek our own vainglory nor further our own name. Grant that we may love and fear and honor you as children do their father.

GOD: How can my name and honor be hallowed in you, while your heart and mind are inclined to evil and are captive to sin, Genesis 8 [:21], Isaiah 52 [:5], and since no one can sing my praise in a foreign land, Psalm 127 [:4]?

The Second Petition

THE SOUL: O Father, that is true. We realize that our members incline to sin and that the world, the flesh, and the devil want to reign in us and thus banish your name and honor from us. Therefore, we ask you to help us out of this misery and to let your kingdom come so that sin may be expelled and we become righteous and acceptable to you, so that you alone may hold sway in us and we may become your kingdom by placing all our powers, both inner and external, in your service.

---

[45] The unusual presentation which follows is a conversation between God, who disturbs and adamantly rejects the petitioner by quoting Scripture, and the petitioner himself, who continues and persists in his supplications.

GOD: Him whom I am to help I destroy. Him whom I want to quicken, save, enrich, and make pious, I mortify, reject, impoverish, and reduce to nothing, Deuteronomy 32 [:39]. However, you refuse to accept such counsel and action from me, Psalm 78 [:10-11]. How, then, am I to help you? And what more can I do? Isaiah 5 [:4].

The Third Petition

THE SOUL: We deplore that we do not understand or accept your helping hand. O Father, grant us your grace and help us to allow your divine will to be done in us. Yes, even though it pains us, continue to punish and stab us, to beat and burn us. Do as you will with us, as long as your will, and not ours, is done. Dear Father, keep us from undertaking and completing anything that is in accord with our own choice, will, and opinion. Your will and ours conflict with each other. Yours alone is good, though it does not seem to be; ours is evil, though it glitters.

GOD: Your lips often voiced your love for me, while your heart was far from me [Isa. 29:13]. And when I chastised you to improve you, you defected; in the midst of my work on you, you deserted me, as you can read in Psalm 78 [:9], "They turned back on the day of battle." Those who made a good beginning and moved me to deal with them turned their backs on me and fell back into sin and into my disfavor.

The Fourth Petition

THE SOUL: O Father, this is very true; "for not by his might shall a man prevail," I Samuel 2 [:9]. And who can abide under your hand if you yourself do not strengthen and comfort us? Therefore, dear Father, seize hold of us, fulfil your will in us so that we may become your kingdom, to your glory and honor. But, dear Father, fortify us in such trials with your holy Word; give us our daily bread. Fashion your dear Son, Jesus Christ, the true heavenly bread, in our hearts so that we, strengthened by him, may cheerfully bear and endure the destruction and death of our will and the perfecting of your will. Yes, grant grace also to all members of Christendom and send us learned priests and pastors who do not feed us the husk and chaff of vain fables, but who teach us your holy gospel and Jesus Christ.

GOD, in Jeremiah 5 and other passages: It is not good to take what is holy and the children's bread and throw it to the dogs [Matt. 7:6; 15:26]. You sin daily, and when I have my Word preached to you day and night, you do not obey and listen, and my Word is despised [Jer. 5:5-6, 21; Isa. 42:20].

The Fifth Petition

THE SOUL: O Father, have mercy on us and do not deny us our precious bread because of that. We are sorry that we do not do justice to your holy Word, and we implore you to have patience with us poor children. Take away our guilt and do not enter into judgment with us, for no one is just in your sight. Remember your promise to forgive those who sincerely forgive their debtors. It is not that we merit your forgiveness because we forgive others, but we know that you are truthful and will graciously forgive all who forgive their neighbors. We place our trust in your promise.

GOD: I forgive and redeem you so often; and you do not remain steadfast and faithful [Ps. 78:8]. You are of weak faith [Matt. 8:26]. You cannot watch and tarry with me a little while, but quickly fall back into temptation. Matthew 26 [:40-41].

The Sixth Petition

THE SOUL: O Father, we are faint and ill, and the trials in the flesh and in the world are severe and manifold. O dear Father, hold us and do not let us fall into temptation and sin again, but give us grace to remain steadfast and fight valiantly to the end. Without your grace and your help, we are not able to do anything.

GOD, in Psalm 11 [:7]: I am just, and my judgment is right. Therefore sin must not go unpunished. Thus you must endure adversity. The fact that trials ensue from this is the fault of your sin, which forces me to punish and curb it.

The Seventh Petition

THE SOUL: Since trials flow from these adversities and tempt us to sin, deliver us, dear Father, from these so that freed from all sin and adversity according to your divine will we may be your kingdom, and laud and praise and hallow you forever. Amen. And since you taught and commanded us to pray thus and have promised fulfilment, we hope and are assured, O dearest Father, that in honor of your truth you will grant all this to us graciously and mercifully.

And finally someone may say, "What am I to do if I cannot believe that I am heard?" Answer: Then follow the example of the father of the child possessed with a dumb spirit. When Christ said to him (as we read in Mark 9 [:23-24]), "Can you believe? All things are possible to him who believes," the father cried with tear-filled eyes, "O Lord, I believe; help my faith if it is too weak!"

To God alone be honor and glory.

ON ROGATIONTIDE PRAYER
AND PROCESSION

1519

Translated by Martin H. Bertram

INTRODUCTION

To counteract the ancient Roman Robigalia,[1] Mamertus, bishop of Vienne, introduced in 473 the observance of Rogation days on the three days between Rogate Sunday and Ascension Day. In 511 the Fifth Council of Orleans made the observance of these Rogation days obligatory for the faithful. On these days worshipers processed out of the cities into the surrounding countryside chanting psalms and litanies. The liturgical color displayed by these processions was violet, to show that it was a penitential season given to fasting and the recitation of penitential litanies. Gradually the emphasis of this observance shifted from one of penitential gratitude for escape from perils to supplication for a good harvest.

In the course of time the observance of Rogation days degenerated into less than a religious celebration. Tippling and disorderly and immoral conduct became associated with the observance and its processions. These abuses afforded Luther another occasion to preach on the subject of prayer. The sermon presented here was preached sometime between May 30 and June 1, 1519, shortly before the debate with John Eck at Leipzig.

Luther's primary aim in this sermon was not to criticize or rail at current abuse, but to remind his hearers how to pray. He who prays, Luther says, must rely upon God's promises and must have no doubt that God is willing and able to hear the supplications offered to him by the faithful. Our own unworthiness is no hindrance to true prayer, nor is our worthiness an asset. We must rely on God's wisdom to give his answer when and as he will, and not seek to lay down our own terms to which we expect God to conform.

The scandalous conduct associated with the Rogation observance, Luther says, has deprived prayer of its true meaning. For this reason both temporal and ecclesiastical authorities should take the necessary steps to purge the observance of its corruption and to

---

[1] This annual festival was observed on April 25 by processions of supplication to the gods of the fields, particularly to Robigus, a god who averted blight.

restore its original penitential character. Prayer in Rogation Week, the Reformer says, should be genuine prayer which does not just implore God's blessing upon the crops, but also asks that through these crops men's souls be nourished.

Two editions of this work appeared in 1519, followed by ten others in 1520 and one in 1522. The translation presented here is based on the text, *Ein Sermon von dem Gebet und Prozession in der Kreuzwoche,*[2] in WA 2, (172) 175-179.

---

[2] The words *Kreuz* ("cross") and *Bitt* ("prayer") were used interchangeably. Rogation days were called both *Kreuzwoche* and *Bittwoche*.

ON ROGATIONTIDE PRAYER
AND PROCESSION

Dr. Martin Luther,
Augustinian Monk in Wittenberg

To begin with, two things are necessary so that a prayer is good and so that it is heard. First, we must have a promise or a pledge from God. We must reflect on this promise and remind God of it, and in that way be emboldened to pray with confidence. If God had not enjoined us to pray and if he had not promised fulfilment, no creature would be able to obtain so much as a kernel of grain[1] despite all his petitions.

It follows from this that no one obtains anything from God by his own virtue or the worthiness of his prayer, but solely by reason of the boundless mercy of God, who, by anticipating all our prayers and desires, induces us through his gracious promise and assurance to petition and to ask so that we might learn how much more he provides for us and how he is more willing to give than we to take or to seek [Eph. 3:20]. He wants to encourage us to pray with confidence, since he offers us more than we are able to ask for.

Second, it is necessary that we never doubt the promise of the truthful and faithful God. The very condition on which he promises fulfilment, yes, the reason he commands us to pray, is so we will be filled with a sure and firm faith that we will be heard. Thus God declares in Matthew 21 [:22] and in Mark 11 [:24], "Therefore I tell you, whatsoever you ask in prayer, believe that you receive it, and you certainly will." And in Luke 11 [:9-13] he says, "And I tell you, ask, and it will be given you; seek, and you will find; knock, and it will be opened to you. Where among you is a son who asks his father for bread, only to have him give him a

---

[1] A direct reference to the great outdoor Rogation festival which initiated the summer planting season.

87

stone? Or if he asks him for a fish, his father gives him a snake? Or if he asks for an egg, he is given a scorpion? If you then, who are not good, are yet able to give good gifts to your children, how much more will the heavenly Father give the good Spirit to those who ask him?" We should cheerfully rely on these and similar promises and commands and pray with true confidence.

Third, if a person prays while doubting God's fulfilment, if he prays without interest[2] in whether or not his prayer is fulfilled, he makes two mistakes. First, he destroys his own prayer and labors in vain. Thus we read in St. James 1 [:6-8], "He who would ask of God, let him so ask that there is no doubt in his faith, for he who doubts is like a wave of the sea that is driven back and forth by the wind. That person must not suppose that he will receive anything from God." James means that God cannot give anything to such a person because that person's heart is unstable. Faith, however, keeps the heart firm and makes it receptive to all God's gifts.

The other mistake is that such a person regards his very faithful and truthful God as a liar and as a fickle and unreliable man who is neither able nor willing to keep his promises. Thus through his doubts he robs God of his honor and of his reputation for faithfulness and truth. This sin is so grave that it changes a person from a Christian into a heathen, into a person who denies and loses his own God. If he persists in this, he will be eternally and hopelessly damned. And if something for which he prayed is granted him, this does not redound to his salvation, but to his temporal and eternal harm. It is not the result of his prayer, but of the wrath of God, who thus rewards the good words which were spoken in sin, unbelief, and divine dishonor.

Fourth, some say, "I would indeed have confidence that my prayer would be answered if I were worthy and possessed merit." I reply: If you refuse to pray until you know or feel yourself worthy and fit you need never pray any more. For as was said before, our prayer must not be based upon or depend upon our worthiness or

---

[2] Luther uses the word *Abenteuer,* related to the Middle High German *aventiure* of the days of knighthood and the English "adventure." The word implies a certain irrational and unconcerned recklessness that is without deep faith.

that of our prayer, but on the unwavering truth of the divine promise. Whenever our prayer is founded on itself or something else, it is false and deceptive, even though it wrings your heart with its intense devotion or weeps sheer drops of blood [Luke 22:44].

We pray after all because we are unworthy to pray. The very fact that we are unworthy and that we dare to pray confidently, trusting only in the faithfulness of God, makes us worthy to pray and to have our prayer answered. Be as unworthy as you may, but know most seriously that it is a thousand times more important, yes, that everything depends on your honoring God's truthfulness and your never giving his promise the lie by your doubts. Your worthiness does not help you; and your unworthiness does not hinder you. Mistrust condemns you, but confidence makes you worthy and upholds you.

All your life you must, therefore, guard against deeming yourself worthy or fit to pray or to receive, unless it be that you proceed with bold courage, trusting in the truthful and certain promises of your gracious God, who thereby wants to reveal his mercy to you. Thus, just as he, unasked, promised fulfilment out of sheer grace to you, an unworthy and undeserving person, he will, in sheer mercy, also give heed to you, an unworthy petitioner. And for all this you have not your own worthiness to thank, but his truth, whereby he has fulfilled his promise, and his mercy, which prompted the promise. This is supported in the statement found in Psalm 25 [:10], "All the works of God are mercy and truth," mercy as manifested in the promise, truth in the keeping and fulfilment of the promise. We also find it in the words of Psalm 85 [:10], "Mercy and truth have kissed," that is, they are joined in every work and gift for which we pray, etc.

Fifth, your trust must not set a goal for God, not set a time and place, not specify the way or the means of his fulfilment, but it must entrust all of that to his will, wisdom, and omnipotence. Just wait cheerfully and undauntedly for the fulfilment without wanting to know how and where, how soon, how late, or by what means. His divine wisdom will find an immeasurably better way and method, time and place, than we can imagine. In fact, even miracles will take place, as in the Old Testament. When the children of Israel trusted in God to redeem them, even though no conceivable possibility was in sight, the Red Sea opened up and afforded them free passage and also drowned all their enemies [Exod. 14:21-29]. Likewise also in Judith 8 [:9-14]: When the holy woman heard that the citizens of Bethulia intended to surrender the city in five days if God would not come to their assistance in the meantime, she rebuked them and said, "Who are you that have put God to the test? By such measures one wins not mercy, but more anger. Do you want to set the time when God will show mercy to you, and determine a day according to your own will?" etc. Therefore, God helped her miraculously so that she beheaded the mighty Holofernes and the enemy was repelled. St. Paul also declares that God is able to do abundantly more and better than we ask or understand [Eph. 3:20]. Hence we must acknowledge that we are too paltry to be able to mention, specify, or suggest time, place, mode, measure, or any other circumstances regarding our requests of God. All this we must leave entirely to the discretion of God and most firmly believe that he will hear us.

Sixth, we must now learn to conduct ourselves properly in Rogation Week and in all processions and litanies. Everyone should see to it that his litany and prayer are in accord with God's name and should petition God with a true and sincere faith, reminding him of his divine and merciful promise. He who is not willing to do that is to remain at home and away from the procession, lest God be more angered by him than appeased by others.

Unfortunately, the processions have become scandalously misused. People want only to see and to be seen in them. They indulge in inane babble and hilarity, to say nothing of even worse conduct and sin. The village processions have become especially disgraceful. These people give themselves to carousing in the taverns. They handle the processional crosses and banners in such a manner that it would not be surprising if God would let us all perish in one year. Things have come to such a pass that there is more valid reason today for entirely abolishing all processions and also the holy days than there ever was for instituting them.[3]

---

[3] See *To the Christian Nobility* (1520), where Luther argues for the abolition of festivals and holy days. *LW* 44, 182-183.

The bishops and also the temporal government should make it their business to remove the abuses or to do away entirely with the processions. It would be far better to gather in the churches for prayer and song than to mock God and his sacred symbols with such impudent behavior. The authorities, both temporal and spiritual, will have to give a grave account for tolerating these abuses or, in the event that they cannot overcome the abuses, for not putting an end to the processions completely. No procession at all is preferable to these.[4]

Seventh, we must pray for two things during the procession and Rogation Week. First, that God may graciously protect the crops in the fields and cleanse the air—not only that God may send blessed rain and good weather to ripen the fruit, but rather that the fruit may not be poisoned, and we, together with the animals, eat and drink thereof and become infected with pestilence, syphilis, fever, and other illnesses. St. Paul declares that "the creatures are blessed and sanctified by the word of God and prayer" [I Tim. 4:4-5]. For where do pestilence and other plagues come from other than from the evil spirits who poison the air and then also the fruit, wine, and grain? And so we, through the sufferance of God, eat and drink death and sickness from our own goods.[5] The Gospels are therefore read publicly in the fields and in the open so that through the power of the holy Word of God the devils may be weakened and the air kept pure and, subsequently, that the fruit may grow vigorously and be a blessing to us. Therefore, we should view the processions and especially the Word of God seriously, devoutly, and with honor and give it ear, firmly believing that the Word of God will exert its power[6] on the fruit and on the air against all

---

[4] On Rogate Sunday, May 21, 1525, Luther stated that "those who first instituted Rogation Week meant well, no doubt, but it has proven to work harm . . . so that the processions were rightly abolished and discontinued." WA 17[I], 248.

[5] Luther here reflects the general medical opinion of his time that evil spirits were the source of illness.

[6] Luther remains logical, for if sickness arises from spirits that are evil, then these can be overcome only by God who is good and by his Word. Luther still displays an almost mystical belief in the magical powers of the Word, broadened in later years by the faith that is required of the individual believer. He also is willing to accept the continued existence of the processions, provided the Word of God is full present.

the princes of the air, that is, the devils, who inhabit the air, as St. Paul says [Eph. 6:12].

Eighth, we should ask God to bless the creatures for us, not merely in the interest of our bodies, as we just heard, but even more for the benefit of our souls, lest the poor soul also be stricken with pestilence and other plagues. This is what I mean: the pestilence and plague of the soul is sin. Whenever God grants us abundant crops in the field, we see how these gifts affect us. Every day we indulge in drunkenness and idleness, followed by unchastity, adultery, cursing, swearing, murder, quarrels, and every other evil, so that it would have been far better if the fields had not been so productive. We then discover that what we asked for in the processions, God gives us abundantly and blesses everything for the welfare of the body, but for the soul all this is a fatal poison and results in the increase of abominable and horrible sin. For to be sated and idle is the greatest plague on earth, the source of all other plagues. No one heeds this pestilence, but we flee from the physical pestilence, pray, and try all kinds of remedies. We willingly enter into this spiritual pestilence, desiring only to have enough earthly goods and to be free of physical pestilence so that we may feast even more on this pestilence and plague. And God, who now sees and recognizes the thoughts of our hearts and our scorn for this plague, closes his eyes and lets matters take their course, gives plentifully to us, blinds us, and immerses us so deeply in our sins that sin thus becomes a habit and a custom, and we no longer regarded it as sin.

In our day there is truly a need for daily processions accompanied by scourging of the body and directed against the visibly rising deluge of all kinds of sin, especially in this country of so much gluttony, tippling, idleness, and what stems from these, in the hope that God might give us grace to use his gifts for our soul's salvation and the betterment of our life, and thus the fruits become the means for maintaining and increasing the health of our body and soul. However, God blinds us so that we do not heed this, but rather use his gifts for the passions of the body and for the soul's eternal damnation. In addition, he gives us a perverted mind so that instead of improving matters we aggravate them and ruin the processions and the day of prayer with our sin. Thus God is angry, and there is no one to stay his anger, while prayer and procession, which should disarm his wrath, serve only to increase it.

May God help us all to come to our senses and to pray in true faith that he may avert his anger. Amen.

A SERMON ON
PREPARING TO DIE

1519

Translated by Martin H. Bertram

INTRODUCTION

Early in May, 1519, Luther's friend George Spalatin forwarded to him the request of a certain Mark Schart[1] that the Reformer give him some help in dealing with distressing thoughts about death. At the time, however, Luther was busy preparing for the debate with John Eck to take place at Leipzig in July.[2] He suggested through Spalatin that Schart read a little book by John Staupitz entitled *The Imitation of the Willing Death of Christ*.[3] On May 18 Luther wrote to Spalatin and again said that he "would be agreeable to Schart's request."[4] On May 24 he wrote again and asked that Schart "be patient,"[5] explaining that the controversies with Eck and Emser[6] were delaying his work on the requested treatise. Four months later in a letter to Spalatin he promised he would write the book "as soon as I can get my breath back again."[7] Finally, on November 1, Luther was able to send printed copies to Spalatin. In an accompanying letter he asked Spalatin to thank Schart for "the ten gulden" and "to send him as many of these little books as you see fit."[8]

---

[1] A counselor at the court of Elector Frederick the Wise, Schart was a large landowner and a generous contributor to the Augustinian monastery and to the University of Wittenberg and its faculty (including Luther) and students. See *Archiv für Reformationsgeschichte*, 8 (1911), 33-34.

[2] See p. 5.

[3] Staupitz (1469-1524) was vicar-general of the Augustinian Order and a close friend of Luther during the Reformer's early years. The book in question was published in Leipzig in 1515. For an example of Luther's high regard for Staupitz, see *LW* 54, 72, 97. For the text of Luther's letter to Spalatin, see *WA*, Br 1, 381.

[4] *WA*, Br 1, 394.

[5] *WA*, Br 1, 407.

[6] On Eck, cf. p. xi and p. 5. Jerome Emser (*ca.* 1477-1527) had, in the course of his early career, taught at the University of Erfurt during Luther's student days there. In 1505 he became secretary to Duke George of Saxony, Luther's bitter foe. After the outbreak of the Reformation Luther and Emser engaged in literary duels, calling each other "the bull of Wittenberg" and "the goat of Leipzig."

[7] *WA*, Br 1, 508.

[8] *LW* 48, 130-131. The ten gulden were a gift from Schart. Luther also remarked that the needs of the poor had made him poorer because "the gulden were given to me because the Lord wanted to help those people" through his loans to them. On the value of the gulden, see *LW* 48, 11, n. 2.

This treatise is another example of Luther's remarkable ability to withdraw from the heat of controversy into the pastoral atmosphere of serene devotion. The entire writing echoes his experience as a pastor and confessor constantly in contact with men and women who were terrified by the maze of popular customs and practices observed by the church in connection with death. To Schart and others like him Luther speaks with intimate and comforting understanding. It was the closeness of death which compelled him into the monastic life.[9] Thus Luther knew what it was to face the mystery and terror of death as a child of his time.[10]

The treatise describes the several stages of preparation for death and strengthens the sufferer's conscience against the temptation to despair because of his sin in the hour of death. Although he still has confidence in the church's sacrament of extreme unction[11] and in prayers addressed to Mary and the saints, the theology of personal faith in Christ emerges clearly.

Within three years this treatise had appeared in twenty-two editions, followed by one in 1523 and another in 1525. The translation presented here is based on the German text, *Ein Sermon von der Bereitung zum Sterben,* in *WA* 2, (680) 685-697. The authenticity of this text is attested by the fact that a copy of this version in the Ducal Library at Wolfenbüttel bears the inscription in Luther's handwriting: "To Mark Schart, my dear friend." [12]

---

[9] See p. ix, n. 1.
[10] Luther often spoke of death both as a medieval man of his times and as an enlightened evangelical. Cf. his *Table Talk. LW* 54, 14-15; 144-145; 190; *et passim.*
[11] See p. 100, n. 2.
[12] *LW* 48, 130, n. 3.

A SERMON ON
PREPARING TO DIE

Martin Luther, Augustinian Monk

First, since death marks a farewell from this world and all its activities, it is necessary that a man regulate his temporal goods properly or as he wishes to have them ordered, lest after his death there be occasion for squabbles, quarrels, or other misunderstanding among his surviving friends. This pertains to the physical or external departure from this world and to the surrender of our possessions.

Second, we must also take leave spiritually. That is, we must cheerfully and sincerely forgive, for God's sake, all men who have offended us. At the same time we must also, for God's sake, earnestly seek the forgiveness of all the people whom we undoubtedly have greatly offended by setting them a bad example or by bestowing too few of the kindnesses demanded by the law of Christian brotherly love. This is necessary lest the soul remain burdened by its actions here on earth.

Third, since everyone must depart, we must turn our eyes to God, to whom the path of death leads and directs us. Here we find the beginning of the narrow gate and of the straight path to life [Matt. 7:14]. All must joyfully venture forth on this path, for though the gate is quite narrow, the path is not long. Just as an infant is born with peril and pain from the small abode of its mother's womb into this immense heaven and earth, that is, into this world, so man departs this life through the narrow gate of death. And although the heavens and the earth in which we dwell at present seem large and wide to us, they are nevertheless much narrower and smaller than the mother's womb in comparison with the future heaven. Therefore, the death of the dear saints is called a new birth, and their feast day is known in Latin as *natale*, that is, the day of their birth.[1] However, the narrow passage of death makes us think of this life as expansive and the life beyond as confined. Therefore, we must believe this and learn a lesson from the physical birth of a child, as Christ declares, "When a woman is in travail she has sorrow; but when she has recovered, she no longer remembers the anguish, since a child is born by her into the world" [John 16:21]. So it is that in dying we must bear this anguish and know that a large mansion and joy will follow [John 14:2].

Fourth, such preparation and readiness for this journey are accomplished first of all by providing ourselves with a sincere confession (of at least the greatest sins and those which by diligent search can be recalled by our memory), with the holy Christian sacrament of the holy and true body of Christ, and with the unction.[2] If these can be had, one should devoutly desire them and receive them with great confidence. If they cannot be had, our longing and yearning for them should nevertheless be a comfort and we should not be too dismayed by this circumstance.[3] Christ says, "All things are possible to him who believes" [Mark 9:23]. The sacraments are nothing else than signs which help and incite us to faith, as we shall see. Without this faith they serve no purpose.

Fifth, we must earnestly, diligently, and highly esteem the holy sacraments, hold them in honor, freely and cheerfully rely on them, and so balance them against sin, death, and hell that they will outweigh these by far. We must occupy ourselves much more with the sacraments and their virtues than with our sins. However, we must know how to give them due honor and we must know what

---

[1] *Natale* (usually spelled *natalis*) dates back to the second century and was observed originally with a religious service commemorating a relative on the anniversary of his death. In the course of time the observance commemorated especially saints and martyrs.

[2] Extreme Unction, one of the seven sacraments of the Roman Catholic Church, is administered to the gravely ill, the dying, or the just deceased. At this point Luther did not openly reject the nonscriptural sacraments. By December, 1519, however, he rejected all the sacraments but penance, baptism, and the Lord's Supper. See his December 18, 1519, letter to Spalatin in WA, Br 1, 594-595. On his views of the sacraments in general, see particularly *The Babylonian Captivity of the Church* (1520). LW 36, 3-126.

[3] Luther expresses a similar view in the case of those who for humanly ordained reasons (i.e., church regulations) are denied the sacrament. See *An Instruction to Penitents* (1521). LW 44, 219-229.

their virtues are. I show them due honor when I believe that I truly receive what the sacraments signify and all that God declares and indicates in them, so that I can say with Mary in firm faith, "Let it be to me according to your words and signs" [Luke 1:38]. Since God himself here speaks and acts through the priest, we would do him in his Word and work no greater dishonor than to doubt whether it is true. And we can do him no greater honor than to believe that his Word and work are true and to firmly rely on them.

Sixth, to recognize the virtues[4] of the sacraments, we must know the evils which they contend with and which we face. There are three such evils: first, the terrifying image of death; second, the awesomely manifold image of sin; third, the unbearable and unavoidable image of hell and eternal damnation.[5] Every other evil issues from these three and grows large and strong as a result of such mingling.

Death looms so large and is terrifying because our foolish and fainthearted nature has etched its image too vividly within itself and constantly fixes its gaze on it. Moreover, the devil presses man to look closely at the gruesome mien and image of death to add to his worry, timidity, and despair. Indeed, he conjures up before man's eyes all the kinds of sudden and terrible death ever seen, heard, or read by man. And then he also slyly suggests the wrath of God with which he [the devil] in days past now and then tormented and destroyed sinners. In that way he fills our foolish human nature with the dread of death while cultivating a love and concern for life, so that burdened with such thoughts man forgets God, flees and abhors death, and thus, in the end, is and remains disobedient to God.

We should familiarize ourselves with death during our lifetime, inviting death into our presence when it is still at a distance

---

[4] In speaking here of virtues and evils, Luther uses the contrasting German words *Tugend* and *Untugend*, today meaning "virtue" and "evil" or "vice." However, just as the English word "virtue" originally meant "strength," so the word *Tugend* (derived from *taugen*, meaning "to be useful" or "to be capable of") in Luther's day implied strength, power, ability, and good characteristics.

[5] The images of which Luther speaks are probably not just theological or symbolic, but allusions to contemporary art exemplified in the works of Dürer and others who depicted dreadful scenes of life in purgatory and hell.

and not on the move. At the time of dying, however, this is hazardous and useless, for then death looms large of its own accord. In that hour we must put the thought of death out of mind and refuse to see it, as we shall hear. The power and might of death are rooted in the fearfulness of our nature and in our untimely and undue viewing and contemplating of it.

Seventh, sin also grows large and important when we dwell on it and brood over it too much. This is increased by the fearfulness of our conscience, which is ashamed before God and accuses itself terribly. That is the water that the devil has been seeking for his mill. He makes our sins seem large and numerous. He reminds us of all who have sinned and of the many who were damned for lesser sins than ours so as to make us despair or die reluctantly, thus forgetting God and being found disobedient in the hour of death. This is true especially since man feels that he should think of his sins at that time and that it is right and useful for him to engage in such contemplation. But he finds himself so unprepared and unfit that now even all his good works are turned into sins. As a result, this must lead to an unwillingness to die, disobedience to the will of God, and eternal damnation. That is not the fitting time to meditate on sin. That must be done during one's lifetime. Thus the evil spirit turns everything upside down for us. During our lifetime, when we should constantly have our eyes fixed on the image of death, sin, and hell—as we read in Psalm 51 [:3], "My sin is ever before me"—the devil closes our eyes and hides these images. But in the hour of death when our eyes should see only life, grace, and salvation, he at once opens our eyes and frightens us with these untimely images so that we shall not see the true ones.

Eighth, hell also looms large because of undue scrutiny and stern thought devoted to it out of season. This is increased immeasurably by our ignorance of God's counsel. The evil spirit prods the soul so that it burdens itself with all kinds of useless presumptions, especially with the most dangerous undertaking of delving into the mystery of God's will to ascertain whether one is "chosen" or not.

Here the devil practices his ultimate, greatest, and most cunning art and power. By this he sets man above God, insofar as man seeks signs of God's will and becomes impatient because he is not supposed to know whether he is among the elect. Man looks with suspicion upon God, so that he soon desires a different God. In brief, the devil is determined to blast God's love from a man's mind and to arouse thoughts of God's wrath. The more docilely man follows the devil and accepts these thoughts, the more imperiled his position is. In the end he cannot save himself, and he falls prey to hatred and blasphemy of God. What is my desire to know whether I am chosen other than a presumption to know all that God knows and to be equal with him so that he will know no more than I do? Thus God is no longer God with a knowledge surpassing mine. Then the devil reminds us of the many heathen, Jews, and Christians who are lost, agitating such dangerous and pernicious thoughts so violently that man, who would otherwise gladly die, now becomes loath to depart this life. When man is assailed by thoughts regarding his election, he is being assailed by hell, as the psalms lament so much.[6] He who surmounts this temptation has vanquished sin, hell, and death all in one.

Ninth, in this affair we must exercise all diligence not to open our homes to any of these images and not to paint the devil over the door.[7] These foes will of themselves boldly rush in and seek to occupy the heart completely with their image, their arguments, and their signs. And when that happens man is doomed and God is entirely forgotten. The only thing to do with these pictures at that time is to combat and expel them. Indeed, where they are found alone and not in conjunction with other pictures, they belong nowhere else than in hell among the devils.

But he who wants to fight against them and drive them out will find that it is not enough just to wrestle and tussle and scuffle with them. They will prove too strong for him, and matters will go from bad to worse. The one and only approach is to drop them entirely and have nothing to do with them. But how is that done? It is done in this way: You must look at death while you are alive and see sin in the light of grace and hell in the light of heaven, permitting nothing to divert you from that view. Adhere to that even

---

[6] Cf. Psalm 65:4; 78:67-68; 106:4-5.
[7] I.e., don't invite the devil's presence.

if all angels, all creatures, yes, even your own thoughts, depict God in a different light—something these will not do. It is only the evil spirit who lends that impression. What shall we do about that?

Tenth, you must not view or ponder death as such, not in yourself or in your nature, nor in those who were killed by God's wrath and were overcome by death. If you do that you will be lost and defeated with them. But you must resolutely turn your gaze, the thoughts of your heart, and all your senses away from this picture and look at death closely and untiringly only as seen in those who died in God's grace and who have overcome death, particularly in Christ and then also in all his saints.

In such pictures death will not appear terrible and gruesome. No, it will seem contemptible and dead, slain and overcome in life. For Christ is nothing other than sheer life, as his saints are likewise. The more profoundly you impress that image upon your heart and gaze upon it, the more the image of death will pale and vanish of itself without struggle or battle. Thus your heart will be at peace and you will be able to die calmly in Christ and with Christ, as we read in Revelation [14:13], "Blessed are they who die in the Lord Christ." This was foreshown in Exodus 21 [Num. 21:6-9], where we hear that when the children of Israel were bitten by fiery serpents they did not struggle with these serpents, but merely had to raise their eyes to the dead bronze serpent and the living ones dropped from them by themselves and perished. Thus you must concern yourself solely with the death of Christ and then you will find life. But if you look at death in any other way, it will kill you with great anxiety and anguish. This is why Christ says, "In the world—that is, in yourselves—you have unrest, but in me you will find peace" [John 16:33].

Eleventh, you must not look at sin in sinners, or in your conscience, or in those who abide in sin to the end and are damned. If you do, you will surely follow them and also be overcome. You must turn your thoughts away from that and look at sin only within the picture of grace. Engrave that picture in yourself with all your power and keep it before your eyes. The picture of grace is nothing else but that of Christ on the cross and of all his dear saints.

How is that to be understood? Grace and mercy are there where Christ on the cross takes your sin from you, bears it for you, and destroys it. To believe this firmly, to keep it before your eyes and not to doubt it, means to view the picture of Christ and to engrave it in yourself. Likewise, all the saints who suffer and die in Christ also bear your sins and suffer and labor for you, as we find it written, "Bear one another's burdens and thus fulfil the command of Christ" [Gal. 6:2]. Christ himself exclaims in Matthew 11 [:28], "Come to me, all who labor and are heavy-laden, and I will help you." In this way you may view your sins in safety without tormenting your conscience. Here sins are never sins, for here they are overcome and swallowed up in Christ. He takes your death upon himself and strangles it so that it may not harm you, if you believe that he does it for you and see your death in him and not in yourself. Likewise, he also takes your sins upon himself and overcomes them with his righteousness out of sheer mercy, and if you believe that, your sins will never work you harm. In that way Christ, the picture of life and of grace over against the picture of death and sin, is our consolation. Paul states that in I Corinthians 15 [:57], "Thanks and praise be to God, who through Christ gives us the victory over sin and death."

Twelfth, you must not regard hell and eternal pain in relation to predestination, not in yourself, or in itself, or in those who are damned, nor must you be worried by the many people in the world who are not chosen. If you are not careful, that picture will quickly upset you and be your downfall. You must force yourself to keep your eyes closed tightly to such a view, for it can never help you, even though you were to occupy yourself with it for a thousand years and fret yourself to death. After all, you will have to let God be God and grant that he knows more about you than you do yourself.

So then, gaze at the heavenly picture of Christ, who descended into hell [I Pet. 3:19] for your sake and was forsaken by God as one eternally damned when he spoke the words on the cross, "Eli, Eli, lama sabachthani!"—"My God, my God, why hast thou forsaken me?" [Matt. 27:46]. In that picture your hell is defeated and your uncertain election is made sure. If you concern yourself solely with that and believe that it was done for you, you will surely be preserved in this same faith. Never, therefore, let this be erased from your vision. Seek yourself only in Christ and not in yourself and you will find yourself in him eternally.

Thus when you look at Christ and all his saints and delight in the grace of God, who elected them, and continue steadfastly in this joy, then you too are already elected. He says in Genesis 12 [:3], "All who bless you shall be blessed." However, if you do not adhere solely to this but have recourse to yourself, you will become adverse to God and all saints, and thus you will find nothing good in yourself. Beware of this, for the evil spirit will strive with much cunning to bring you to such a pass.

Thirteenth, these three pictures or conflicts are foreshadowed in Judges 7 [:16-22], where we read that Gideon attacked the Midianites at night with three hundred men in three different places, but did no more than have trumpets blown and glass fragments smashed. The foe fled and destroyed himself. Similarly, death, sin, and hell will flee with all their might if in the night we but keep our eyes on the glowing picture of Christ and his saints and abide in the faith, which does not see and does not want to see the false pictures. Furthermore, we must encourage and strengthen ourselves with the Word of God as with the sound of trumpets.

Isaiah [9:4] introduces this same figure very aptly against these three images, saying of Christ, "For the yoke of his burden, and the staff for his shoulder, the rod of his oppressor, thou hast broken as in the days of the Midianites," who were overcome by Gideon. He says as it were: The sins of your people (which are a heavy "yoke of his burden" for his conscience), and death (which is a "staff" or punishment laid upon his shoulder), and hell (which is a powerful "rod of the oppressor" with which eternal punishment for sin is exacted)—all these you have broken and defeated. This came to pass in the days of Gideon, that is, when Gideon, by faith and without wielding his sword, put his enemies to flight.

And when did Christ do this? On the cross! There he prepared himself as a threefold picture for us, to be held before the eyes of our faith against the three evil pictures with which the evil spirit and our nature would assail us to rob us of this faith. He is the

living and immortal image against death, which he suffered, yet by
his resurrection from the dead he vanquished death in his life. He
is the image of the grace of God against sin, which he assumed,
and yet overcame by his perfect obedience. He is the heavenly
image, the one who was forsaken by God as damned, yet he conquered hell through his omnipotent love, thereby proving that he
is the dearest Son, who gives this to us all if we but believe.

Fourteenth, beyond all this he not only defeated sin, death,
and hell in himself and offered his victory to our faith, but for our
further comfort he himself suffered and overcame the temptation
which these pictures entail for us. He was assailed by the images
of death, sin, and hell just as we are. The Jews confronted Christ
with death's image when they said, "Let him come down from the
cross; he has healed others, let him now help himself" [Matt. 27:
40-42]. They said as it were, "Here you are facing death; now you
must die; nothing can save you from that." Likewise, the devil holds
the image of death before the eyes of a dying person and frightens
his fearful nature with this horrible picture.

The Jews held the image of sin before Christ's eyes when they
said to him, "He healed others. If he is the Son of God, let him
come down from the cross, etc."—as though they were to say, "His
works were all fraud and deception. He is not the Son of God but
the son of the devil, whose own he is with body and soul. He never
worked any good, only iniquity." And just as the Jews cast these
three pictures at Christ in wild confusion, so man too is assailed
by all three at the same time in disarray to bewilder him and ultimately to drive him to despair. The Lord describes the destruction
of Jerusalem in Luke 19 [:43-44], saying that the city's enemies
will surround it with such devastation as to cut off escape—that is
death. Furthermore, he says that its enemies will terrify the inhabi-
tants and drive them hither and yon so that they will not know
where to turn—that is sin. In the third place, he says that the foe
will dash them to the ground and not leave one stone upon another
—that is hell and despair.

The Jews pressed the picture of hell before Christ's eyes when
they said, "He trusts in God; let us see whether God will deliver
him now, for he said he is the Son of God" [Matt. 27:43]—as though

they were to say, "His place is in hell; God did not elect him; he is rejected forever. All his confidence and hope will not help him. All is in vain."

And now we mark that Christ remained silent in the face of all these words[8] and horrible pictures. He does not argue with his foes; he acts as though he does not hear or see them and makes no reply. Even if he had replied, he would only have given them cause to rave and rant even more horribly. He is so completely devoted to the dearest will of his Father that he forgets about his own death, his sin, and his hell imposed on him, and he intercedes for his enemies, for their sin, death, and hell [Luke 23:34]. We must, similarly, let these images slip away from us to wherever they wish or care to go, and remember only that we cling to God's will, which is that we hold to Christ and firmly believe our sin, death, and hell are overcome in him and no longer able to harm us. Only Christ's image must abide in us. With him alone we must confer and deal.

Fifteenth, we now turn to the holy sacraments and their blessings to learn to know their benefits and how to use them. Anyone who is granted the time and the grace to confess, to be absolved, and to receive the sacrament and Extreme Unction before his death has great cause indeed to love, praise, and thank God and to die cheerfully, if he relies firmly on and believes in the sacraments, as we said earlier. In the sacraments your God, Christ himself, deals, speaks, and works with you through the priest. His are not the works and words of man. In the sacraments God himself grants you all the blessings we just mentioned in connection with Christ. God wants the sacraments to be a sign and testimony that Christ's life has taken your death, his obedience your sin, his love your hell, upon themselves and overcome them. Moreover, through the same sacraments you are included and made one with all the saints. You thereby enter into the true communion of saints so that they die with you in Christ, bear sin, and vanquish hell.

It follows from this that the sacraments, that is, the external words of God as spoken by a priest, are a truly great comfort and at the same time a visible sign of divine intent. We must cling to

---

[8] According to Matthew, Jesus spoke only once during his agony on the cross. See Matt. 27:46.

them with a staunch faith as to the good staff which the patriarch Jacob used when crossing the Jordan [Gen. 32:10], or as to a lantern by which we must be guided, and carefully walk with open eyes the dark path of death, sin, and hell, as the prophet says, "Thy word is a light to my feet" [Ps. 119:105]. St. Peter also declares, "And we have a sure word from God. You will do well to pay attention to it" [II Pet. 1:19]. There is no other help in death's agonies, for everyone who is saved is saved only by that sign. It points to Christ and his image, enabling you to say when faced by the image of death, sin, and hell, "God promised and in his sacraments he gave me a sure sign of his grace that Christ's life overcame my death in his death, that his obedience blotted out my sin in his suffering, that his love destroyed my hell in his forsakenness. This sign and promise of my salvation will not lie to me or deceive me. It is God who has promised it, and he cannot lie either in words or in deeds." He who thus insists and relies on the sacraments will find that his election and predestination will turn out well wihout his worry and effort.[9]

Sixteenth, it is of utmost importance that we highly esteem, honor, and rely upon the holy sacraments, which contain nothing but God's words, promises, and signs. This means that we have no doubts about the sacraments or the things of which they are certain signs, for if we doubt these we lose everything. Christ says that it will happen to us as we believe.[10] What will it profit you to assume and to believe that sin, death, and hell are overcome in Christ for others, but not to believe that your sin, your death, and your hell are also vanquished and wiped out and that you are thus redeemed? Under those circumstances the sacraments will be completely fruitless, since you do not believe the things which are indicated, given, and promised there to you. That is the vilest sin that can be committed, for God himself is looked upon as a liar in his Word, signs, and works, as one who speaks, shows, and promises something which he neither means nor intends to keep. Therefore we dare not

---

[9] In contrast to the Roman church, which emphasized what Luther called the "monster of uncertainty," Luther stressed the certainty of salvation for him who believes and trusts in the truth of the sacraments. Cf. WA 40^I, 588; WA 48, 227.

[10] Matt. 15:28; 21.

trifle with the sacraments. Faith must be present for a firm reliance and cheerful venturing on such signs and promises of God. What sort of a God or Savior would he be who could not or would not save us from sin, death, and hell? Whatever the true God promises and effects must be something big.

But then the devil comes along and whispers into your ear, "But suppose you received the sacraments unworthily and through your unworthiness robbed yourself of such grace?" [11] In that event cross yourself[12] and do not let the question of your worthiness or unworthiness assail you. Just see to it that you believe that these are sure signs, true words of God, and then you will indeed be and remain worthy. Belief makes you worthy; unbelief makes you unworthy. The evil spirit brings up the question of worthiness and unworthiness to stir up doubts within you, thus nullifying the sacraments with their benefits and making God a liar in what he says.

God gives you nothing because of your worthiness, nor does he build his Word and sacraments on your worthiness, but out of sheer grace he establishes you, unworthy one, on the foundation of his Word and signs. Hold fast to that and say, "He who gives and has given me his signs and his Word, which assure me that Christ's life, grace, and heaven have kept my sin, death, and hell from harming me, is truly God, who will surely preserve these things for me. When the priest absolves me, I trust in this as in God's Word itself. Since it is God's Word, it must come true. That is my stand, and on that stand I will die." You must trust in the priest's absolution as firmly as though God had sent a special angel or apostle to you, yes, as though Christ himself were absolving you.

Seventeenth, we must note that he who receives the sacraments has a great advantage, for he has received a sign and a promise from God with which he can exercise and strengthen his belief that he has been called into Christ's image and to his benefits. The others who must do without these signs labor solely in faith and must obtain these benefits with the desires of their hearts. They will, of course, also receive these benefits if they persevere in that

---

[11] Cf. Luther's discussion of this point on pp. 174-175.
[12] Signing or blessing oneself with the sign of the cross was, among other things, an affirmation of the power of Christ aainst evil spirits and demons.

same faith. Thus you must also say with regard to the Sacrament of the Altar, "If the priest gave me the holy body of Christ, which is a sign and promise of the communion of all angels and saints that they love me, provide and pray for me, suffer and die with me, bear my sin and overcome hell, it will and must therefore be true that the divine sign does not deceive me. I will not let anyone rob me of it. I would rather deny all the world and myself than doubt my God's trustworthiness and truthfulness in his signs and promises. Whether worthy or unworthy of him, I am, according to the text and the declaration of this sacrament, a member of Christendom. It is better that I be unworthy than that God's truthfulness be questioned. Devil, away with you if you advise me differently."

Just see how many people there are who would like to be certain or to have a sign from heaven to tell them how they stand with God and whether they are elected. But what help would it be to them to receive such a sign if they would still not believe? What good are all the signs without faith? How did Christ's signs and the apostles' signs help the Jews? What help are the venerable signs of the sacraments and the words of God even today? Why do people not hold to the sacraments, which are sure and appointed signs, tested and tried by all saints and found reliable by all who believed and who received all that they indicate?

We should, then, learn what the sacraments are, what purpose they serve, and how they are to be used. We will find that there is no better way on earth to comfort downcast hearts and bad consciences. In the sacraments we find God's Word—which reveals and promises Christ to us with all his blessing and which he himself is—against sin, death, and hell. Nothing is more pleasing and desirable to the ear than to hear that sin, death, and hell are wiped out. That very thing is effected in us through Christ if we see the sacraments properly.

The right use of the sacraments involves nothing more than believing that all will be as the sacraments promise and pledge through God's Word. Therefore, it is necessary not only to look at the three pictures in Christ and with these to drive out the counter-pictures, but also to have a definite sign which assures us that this has surely been given to us. That is the function of the sacraments.

Eighteenth, in the hour of his death no Christian should doubt that he is not alone. He can be certain, as the sacraments point out, that a great many eyes are upon him: first, the eyes of God and of Christ himself, for the Christian believes his words and clings to his sacraments; then also, the eyes of the dear angels, of the saints, and of all Christians. There is no doubt, as the Sacrament of the Altar indicates, that all of these in a body run to him as one of their own, help him overcome sin, death, and hell, and bear all things with him. In that hour the work of love and the communion of saints are seriously and mightily active. A Christian must see this for himself and have no doubt regarding it, for then he will be bold in death. He who doubts this does not believe in the most venerable Sacrament of the Body of Christ, in which are pointed out, promised, and pledged the communion, help, love, comfort, and support of all the saints in all times of need. If you believe in the signs and words of God, his eyes rest upon you, as he says in Psalm 32 [:8], "*Firmabo*, etc., my eyes will constantly be upon you lest you perish." If God looks upon you, all the angels, saints, and all creatures will fix their eyes upon you. And if you remain in that faith, all of them will uphold you with their hands. And when your soul leaves your body, they will be on hand to receive it, and you cannot perish.

This is borne out in the person of Elisha, who according to II Kings 6 [:16-17] said to his servant, "Fear not, for those who are with us are more than those who are with them." This he said although enemies had surrounded them and they could see nothing but these. The Lord opened the eyes of the young man, and they were surrounded by a huge mass of horses and chariots of fire.

The same is true of everyone who trusts God. Then the words found in Psalm 34 [:7] apply, "The angel of the Lord will encamp around those who fear him, and deliver them." And in Psalm 125 [:1-2], "Those who trust in the Lord are like Mount Zion, which cannot be moved, but abides forever. As the mountains (that is, the angels) are round about Jerusalem, so the Lord is round about his people, from this time forth and forevermore." And in Psalm 91 [:11-16], "For he has charged his angels to bear you on their hands and to guard you wherever you go lest you dash your foot against a stone. You will tread on the lion and the adder, the young lion and the serpent you will trample under foot (this means that all the power and the cunning of the devil will be unable to harm you), because he has trusted in me and I will deliver him; I will protect him because he knows my name. When he calls to me, I will answer him; I will be with him in all his trials, I will rescue him and honor him. With eternal life will I satisfy him, and show him my eternal grace."

Thus the Apostle also declares that the angels, whose number is legion, are all ministering spirits and are sent out for the sake of those who are to be saved [Heb. 1:14]. These are all such great matters that who can believe them? Therefore, we must know that even though the works of God surpass human understanding, God yet effects all of this through such insignificant signs as the sacraments to teach us what a great thing a true faith in God really is.

Nineteenth, let no one presume to perform such things by his own power, but humbly ask God to create and preserve such faith in and such understanding of his holy sacraments in him. He must practice awe and humility in all this, lest he ascribe these works to himself instead of allowing God the glory. To this end he must call upon the holy angels, particularly his own angel,[13] the Mother of God, and all the apostles and saints,[14] especially since God has granted him exceptional zeal for this. However, he dare not doubt, but must believe that his prayer will be heard. He has two reasons for this. The first one is that he has just heard from the Scriptures how God commanded the angels to give love and help to all who believe and how the sacrament conveys this. We must hold this before them and remind them of it, not that the angels do not know this, or would otherwise not do it, but to make our faith and trust in them, and through them in God, stronger and bolder as we face death. The other reason is that God has enjoined us firmly to believe in the fulfilment of our prayer [Mark 11:24] and that it is truly an Amen.[15] We must also bring this command of God to his

---

[13] On guardian angels, see Gal. 1:8; I Tim. 3:16; 1 Pet. 1:12.
[14] On Luther's later opposition to the invocation of Mary and the saints, see *On Translating: An Open Letter* (1530). LW 35, 198-200.
[15] See Luther's treatment of "Amen" on pp. 76-77.

attention and say, "My God, you have commanded me to pray and to believe that my prayer will be heard. For this reason I come to you in prayer and am assured that you will not forsake me but will grant me a genuine faith."

Moreover, we should implore God and his dear saints our whole life long for true faith in the last hour, as we sing so very fittingly on the day of Pentecost, "Now let us pray to the Holy Spirit for the true faith of all things the most, that in our last moments he may befriend us, and as home we go, he may tend us." [16] When the hour of death is at hand we must offer this prayer to God and, in addition, remind him of his command and of his promise and not doubt that our prayer will be fulfilled. After all, if God commanded us to pray and to trust in prayer, and, furthermore, has granted us the grace to pray, why should we doubt that his purpose in this was also to hear and to fulfil it?

Twentieth, what more should God do to persuade you to accept death willingly and not to dread but to overcome it? In Christ he offers you the image of life, of grace, and of salvation so that you may not be horrified by the images of sin, death, and hell. Furthermore, he lays your sin, your death, and your hell on his dearest Son, vanquishes them, and renders them harmless for you. In addition, he lets the trials of sin, death, and hell that come to you also assail his Son and teaches you how to preserve yourself in the midst of these and how to make them harmless and bearable. And to relieve you of all doubt, he grants you a sure sign, namely, the holy sacraments. He commands his angels, all saints, all creatures to join him in watching over you, to be concerned about your soul, and to receive it. He commands you to ask him for this and to be assured of fulfilment. What more can or should he do?

From this you can see that he is a true God and that he performs great, right, and divine works for you. Why, then, should he not impose something big upon you (such as dying), as long as he adds to it great benefits, help, and strength, and thereby wants to test the power of his grace. Thus we read in Psalm 111 [:2],

---

[16] Luther quotes a well-known hymn of which he thought very highly. He later translated it into German and added three verses of his own composition. See *LW* 53, 263-264 for the full text.

"Great are the works of the Lord, selected according to his pleasure." Therefore, we ought to thank him with a joyful heart for showing us such wonderful, rich, and immeasurable grace and mercy against death, hell, and sin, and to laud and love his grace rather than fearing death so greatly. Love and praise make dying very much easier, as God tells us through Isaiah, "For the sake of my praise I restrain it [wrath] for you, that I may not cut you off." [17] To that end may God help us. Amen.

---

[17] Isa. 48:9 (RSV). Luther actually uses a more literal translation of the original and says of God, who is willing to forgo being honored by his people, "I shall curb your mouth in its praise of me, so that you will not perish." Cf. WA 2, 697.

FOURTEEN CONSOLATIONS

1520

Translated by Martin H. Bertram

INTRODUCTION

Upon his return from the 1519 Imperial Diet, at which Charles of Spain was elected Holy Roman Emperor, Saxon Elector Frederick the Wise[1] became so ill that there was widespread doubt he would recover. In view of these circumstances George Spalatin, court chaplain and a friend of Luther, urged Luther to prepare some writing of spiritual comfort for their common sovereign. Indebted to the Elector for firm and unyielding protection against his enemies, Luther felt a special sense of obligation to comply with Spalatin's suggestion.

The structure of the writing derives from a cult popular in medieval Germany. According to the legend behind the cult, a Franconian shepherd in 1446 had a vision of the Christ Child surrounded by fourteen saints. In the course of time the fourteen saints acquired names and each became identified as a protector against a particular disease.[2] Luther devised fourteen consolations arranged in the form of a reredos or altar screen similar to the altar screens depicting the fourteen saints.[3] Luther thus effects a literary altar screen, the first panel or section of which is devoted to the contemplation of seven evils; the second, to the contemplation of seven blessings which God's grace bestows upon the faithful believer.

---

[1] Frederick III, called "the Wise" (1463-1525), was a model medieval Catholic prince. He refused, however, to surrender Luther to Rome and extended his protection to the Wittenberg professor, who was his subject.
[2] The fourteen saints were: Denis of Paris (headache and rabies); Erasmus, called Elmo (colic and cramp); Blaise (throat ailments); Barbara (lightning, fire, explosion, sudden and evil death); Margaret (demonic possession and for pregnant women); Catherine of Alexandria (philosophers, students); George (soldiers); Achatius and Eustace (hunters); Pantaleon the Physician (tuberculosis); Giles (epilepsy, sterility, insanity); Cyriac the Deacon (demonic possession); Vitus the Martyr (epilepsy); Christopher the Giant (travelers). Various areas substituted local saints for some of those listed here. The plague years of the fourteenth century may have helped to promote the cult. *New Catholic Encyclopedia* (New York: McGraw-Hill Book Company, 1967), V, 1045-1046.
[3] The basic theme or approach of the writing is rooted in Ecclus. 11:25 (see p. 124). As for the specific form and arrangement of the work, Luther may have had in mind some particular altar painting of the fourteen saints. Such a painting by Lucas Cranach hung in the Torgau residence of the Elector. Significantly, it was at Torgau that the Elector lay critically ill. See PE 1, 107.

The intent of the contemplation of the seven evils is to show the relative insignificance of present evils in comparison, for example, with the evils a sinner justly deserves, and with the sufferings endured by Christ on the cross. By the same token, the contemplation of God's great blessings here and hereafter will enable the believer to dismiss as nothing the sufferings he presently must undergo.

Luther began work on this little book early in August, 1519, and completed it on or shortly after August 29. On September 22 he sent the Latin manuscript to Spalatin with the request that he prepare a free German translation for the ailing Elector. Spalatin completed his translation by the end of November[4] and returned the original Latin manuscript to Luther. From the very first Luther had intended this writing solely for the Elector. Upon Spalatin's insistence, however, he published both the Latin and German versions at Wittenberg in February, 1520. The German edition included a letter of dedication addressed to Frederick; the Latin edition, due to an oversight of the printer, omitted it.

Numerous editions of the work were published, often by other people. During the winter of 1535/36 Luther himself oversaw the publication of a new edition, to which he added both a preface and the Latin dedication which had been omitted in the 1520 edition published at Wittenberg. Significantly, as Luther himself explains,[5] he did not alter or delete those passages which in later years he would reject.

As early as 1578 an English translation appeared, followed by another edition in 1580.[6] Henry Cole included it in his *Select Works of Martin Luther*, published in 1824.[7] The translation presented here is based on the Latin text, *Tessaradecas Consolatoria pro laborantibus et onerantis*, in WA 6, (99) 104-134.

---

[4] In view of the seriousness of the Elector's illness, it seems strange that there was such leisureliness about the project. A. T. W. Steinhaeuser suggests that Luther may have transmitted the manuscript to the Elector in instalments. See *PE* 1, 105.

[5] See p. 121.

[6] W. Gace (trans.), *A right comfortable Treatise conteining sundrye pointes of consolation for them that labour and are laden.* See *PE* 1, 107, n. 3.

[7] London; II, 123-176.

FOURTEEN CONSOLATIONS

For Those who Labor and Are Heavy-laden
by Martin Luther, Augustinian of Wittenberg

Preface[1]

This book was written at the beginning of the movement started by me[2] for the most excellent prince, Frederick, duke of Saxony, when he was stricken with a grave illness.[3] However, since it appealed to many, it was printed. Because it was falsified and mutilated in many editions so that even I could no longer remember many of the passages as they had been written, I have restored the sense of them as well as I could, and I believe they represent the views I held at the beginning. I do not intend to alter or improve the thoughts, as I well might do. In this book I want to give proof of my progress and also please my adversaries by giving them something on which they can vent their malice. It is enough for me if I please my Lord Christ and his saints. The fact that I am hated by the devil and his scaly ones[4] makes me rejoice with all my heart and give thanks to my God.

Letter of Dedication

To the Most Illustrious Prince and Lord, Frederick, duke of Saxony, arch-marshal and elector of the Holy Roman Empire, landgrave of Thuringia, margrave of Meissen, His Most Gracious Lord.

Our Lord and Savior Jesus has left us a commandment which applies equally to all Christians, namely, that we are to render hu-

---

[1] The Preface, of course, was not in Luther's original Latin manuscript. See p. 120.
[2] I.e., the Reformation.
[3] Cf. p. 119.
[4] I.e., Luther's opponents, whom he regarded as disciples of the devil.

manitarian services, or rather (as the Scriptures call them), the works of mercy [Luke 6:36], to those who are afflicted and in a state of calamity, and that we are to visit the sick, try to free the captives, and do similar things for our neighbor so that the evils of the present may be somewhat lessened. Our Lord Jesus Christ himself gave us the brightest example of this commandment when, because of his infinite love for the race of men, he descended from the bosom of the Father into our misery and our prison, that is, into our flesh and our most wretched life, and took upon himself the penalty for our sins so that we might be saved, as he says in Isaiah 43 [:24], "You have burdened me with your sins, and you have wearied me with your iniquities."

He who is not moved by this illustrious example and is not driven by the authority of the divine commandment to do such works of mercy will, at the last judgment, deserve to hear the voice of the angry judge, saying, "Depart from me, you cursed ones, into everlasting fire. I was sick, and you did not visit me. With gross ingratitude for the supreme blessings bestowed by me upon you and the whole world, you have not by even the smallest service come to aid your brethren—no, me, Christ, your God and Savior, in the brethren" [Matt. 25:41-45].

Thus, Most Illustrious Prince, since I saw that your Lordship has been stricken with a grave illness and that Christ also is sick in you, I have deemed it my duty to visit your Lordship with this little writing. I cannot pretend that I do not hear the voice of Christ as it cries to me out of your Lordship's body and flesh, saying, "Look, I am sick." Such evils as sickness and the like are borne not by us Christians, but by Christ himself, our Lord and Savior, in whom we live and who plainly testifies in the Gospel, "Whatever you have done unto the least of mine, you have done unto me" [Matt. 25:40]. And while we have the duty to visit and console all who are afflicted with sickness, we are especially obligated to those of the household of faith. Paul clearly distinguishes between strangers and those of the household, those bound to us by intimate ties, Galatians 6 [:10].

But I also have other reasons for performing this my duty. I realize that as one of your Lordship's subjects, I should share in your Lordship's illness together with the rest of your subjects, and suffer with you, as a member with its head [Rom. 12:5], on whom all our fortunes, all our safety and happiness, depend. We recognize in your Lordship another Naaman, by whom God is now giving deliverance to Germany, as in times past he gave deliverance through him to Syria [II Kings 5:1]. Therefore, the whole Roman Empire turns its eyes only to your Lordship and venerates and admires you as the father of the fatherland, as the symbol of the entire empire, as the armament and protector, particularly of the German nation.

However, we are bound not only to console your Lordship with all our powers and to make your condition our own, but also much more to pray to God for your safety and health, which I hope is being done with all diligence and devotion by your Lordship's subjects. But as for me, whom your Lordship's many and signal benefactions have made your debtor above all others, I recognize it to be my duty to express my gratitude by rendering some special service. But since because of my poverty both of mind and fortune, I can offer nothing of value, Doctor George Spalatin, one of your Lordship's chaplains, opportunely suggested to me that I prepare and present to your Lordship a spiritual consolation, and that such a service would be most acceptable to your Lordship. Being unwilling to reject this friendly counsel, I have put together these fourteen chapters after the fashion of an altar screen[5] and have given them the name *Fourteen Consolations*. They are to replace the fourteen saints whom our superstition has invented and called "The Defenders Against All Evils."[6] Now this is a spiritual screen and not made of silver. The book is not meant to adorn the walls of churches, but to uplift and strengthen the pious heart. I trust that it will be a great help to your Lordship in your present condition. The book consists of two parts: the first part deals with the seven images of evil, a contemplation of which will make the troubles of the present lighter. The second part also has seven images, but of blessings, gathered together for the same purpose.

May it please your Lordship graciously to accept this little

---

[5] Cf. p. 119.
[6] Cf. p. 119, n. 2.

work of mine and make such use of it that the diligent reading and contemplation of these images may bring some comfort. I humbly commend myself to your Lordship.

Your subject,

MARTIN LUTHER, Doctor

Introduction

In speaking of the consolation which Christians have, the Apostle Paul in Romans 15 [:4] writes, "Brethren, whatever was written, was written for our instruction, so that through the patience and comfort of the Scriptures we might have hope." In this passage he plainly teaches us that our consolations are to be drawn from the Holy Scriptures.

The Holy Scriptures approach the matter of comfort in a twofold manner, insofar as they present to our view both blessings and evils, wholesomely intermingled. This is in accord with the word of the Preacher, "In the day of evil be mindful of the good, and in the day of the good be mindful of the evil" [Ecclus. 11:25]. The Holy Spirit knows that a thing has only such value and meaning to a man as he assigns to it in his thoughts. Whatever he regards as trivial and of no value will affect him only slightly, whether it be love when it comes to him or pain when it goes away. Therefore, the Spirit tries with great effort to draw man away from thinking about things and from being affected by them. When he has accomplished this, then man is indifferent about things no matter what they may be. Therefore, the diversion is best effected through the Word, by which our present thought is turned from the thing that moves us at the present moment to something that is either absent or does not move us at the moment. It is thus very true that we shall find consolation only through the Scriptures, which in the days of evil call us to the contemplation of our blessings, either present or to come, and, in the days of blessing, point us to the contemplation of the evils.

For a better understanding of these two series of pictures or images, let us divide each into seven parts.

124

The first part will deal with the evils. First we shall consider the evil within us; second, the evil before us; third, the evil behind us; fourth, the evil on our left hand; fifth, the evil on our right hand; sixth, the evil beneath us; and seventh, the evil above us.[7]

Chapter One: The First Image

The Evil Within Us

Whether man believes it or not, it is most certain and true that no torture can compare with the worst of all evils, namely, the evil within man himself. The evils within him are more numerous and far greater than any which he feels. If a man were to feel his evil, he would feel hell, for he has hell within himself. You ask, "How can that be?" The prophet says, "All men are liars" [Ps. 116:11], and again, "Every man living is nothing but vanity" [Ps. 39:6]. But to be a liar and a vanity is to be without truth and reality. And to be without truth and reality is to be without God and to be nothing. This condition in turn is to be in hell and to be damned.

Therefore, when God in his mercy chastens us, he shows us and lays upon us only the lighter evils, for God knows that if he were to lead a man to a full knowledge of his own evils, that man would die at once. He did, however, give a taste of this to some, of whom it is said, "He brings down to hell and brings back again" [I Sam. 2:6]. Therefore, they speak the truth who say that our physical sufferings are monitors of the evil within. In Hebrews 12 [:6], the Apostle calls them God's fatherly chastenings when he says, "He scourges every son whom he receives." By such scourgings and lesser evils he drives out those great evils, which we will then not need to feel, as it is written in Proverbs 22 [:15], "Foolishness is bound up in the heart of a child, but the rod of discipline shall drive it away." Do not loving parents grieve more for their sons who are thieves and evildoers than when they are wounded in their

---

[7] Luther, however, does not follow this sequence in the development of the work.

125

body? In fact, they themselves beat and hurt them to keep them from becoming evildoers.[8]

What is it, then, that prevents us from feeling this true evil? As I have said, it is because God has so ordered things that man might not perish by seeing his innermost evils. God hides them and wants us to see them only by faith, when he points them out by the evil that is felt. Therefore, in the day of evils remember the day of blessings [Ecclus. 11:25]. Just see what a great good it is not to know the whole of our evil. Be mindful of this good, and the evil that you feel will torment you less. On the other hand, in the day of good be mindful of the evil. That is to say, while you do not feel the true evils, be grateful that you do not, but keep the true evils in mind. The evil that you feel will then be less of a burden. It is therefore clear that in this life a man's freedom from pain is always greater than his pain. This is not because his whole evil is not present, but because the goodness of God keeps it hidden so that he neither thinks of it nor feels it.

Thus we observe how those to whom their true evil has been revealed rage furiously against themselves, how they count whatever suffering life may bring as nothing, as long as they need not feel their own pain. Everyone who felt or firmly believed in the evil within himself would do the same. He would voluntarily invite all external evils, hold them to be mere child's play, and would never be more sad than when he had no evils to bear. We know that this was true of some saints, for example, David in Psalm 6.

Therefore, the first image becomes a consolation when a man says to himself, "Not yet, O man, do you feel your evil. Be glad and grateful that you do not have to feel it." When compared with the greatest evil, the small evil thus becomes light. It is this that others mean when they say, "I have deserved something far worse, even hell itself"—a thing so easy to say, but horrible to endure.

Although this evil is hidden deeply, it bears fruits which are

---

[8] A. T. W. Steinhaeuser suggests that Luther here was remembering the severity of his parents. *PE* 1, 116, n. 1. For the specific recollection, see *LW* 54, 235.

clearly seen. These are the dread and uncertainty of a trembling conscience, when faith is assailed and a man is not sure or is in doubt whether he has a gracious God. The weaker a man's faith, the more bitter will be the fruit. When viewed rightly, this one weakness alone, since it is spiritual, outweighs by far the weakness of the body, and a careful comparison makes it seem very light indeed.

Beyond this but part of the evils within us are all those tragic experiences described by the Preacher when he refers again and again to "vanity and vexation of the spirit" [Eccles. 1:2, 14]. How many of our plans end in frustration! How many of our hopes are dashed! How many things do we see, how many do we hear that we do not like! And the very things that happen in accord with our wish also happen against our wish. Nothing is complete and perfect. Finally, all these things are so much greater the higher one rises in station and rank.[9] Such a person will of necessity be driven about by far more and greater billows, floods, and tempests than others in a similar situation. Thus Psalm 104 [:25] says rightly, "In the sea of this world there are small and large animals, creeping beings without number," that is, an infinite number of trials. This is why Job [7:1] calls the life of man "a trial."

Yet these do not cease being evils just because they are less sharply felt by us. But because they are always with us and always active they have lost some of their meaning, and because of the goodness of God our thoughts and feelings about them are blunted. They affect us more powerfully when we have not learned to despise them through familiarity with them. It is very true that we feel scarcely a thousandth part of our evils. And it is equally true that we measure, feel, or do not feel our evils not on the basis of the facts, but on the basis of our own thoughts and feelings.

Chapter Two: The Second Image

The Future Evil or the Evil Before Us

It will lighten your present evil in no small degree if you will turn your mind to the future evils. These are so numerous, so

---

[9] Luther here and below has Elector Frederick specifically in mind.

varied, and so great that they have given rise to one of the great and principal emotions, namely, fear. Fear has been defined by some as the emotion that is caused by a future evil. Therefore the Apostle says in Romans 11 [:20], "Be not proud, but rather fear." This evil increases because of our uncertainty as to the form and force that it will assume. This has resulted in the common saying, "No age is proof against the itch," although this is a disease only of children and infants. Even so, no man is safe from the evils that befall any other, for what one has suffered another may also suffer. This applies to all the historic events and tragedies of all ages and to all the lamentations of the world. This applies also to the more than three hundred diseases which have been observed and with which the human body can be afflicted. And if there are that many diseases, how great do you think will be the number of the misfortunes that assail our possessions, our friends, and even our very mind, which, after all, is the main target of all evils and the one trysting place of sorrow and every ill?

These evils increase in power and intensity as a man rises to higher dignity and rank. Since misery, shame, and indignity can suddenly overtake a man of such an exalted estate, he must at all times be in dread of these evils, for they all hang by but a slender thread, like the sword which the tyrant Dionysius suspended above the head of his guest at his table.

If none of these evils befalls us, we should consider this a gain and no small comfort in the evil that does in fact become our lot, and exclaim with Jeremiah, "It is of the Lord's mercies that we are not consumed" [Lam. 3:22]. When none of these things happens to us it is because the preventing right hand of the Most High surrounds us on all sides with great might and like a wall (as is seen in the case of Job), so that Satan and the evils in their frustration can only be grievously vexed. From this we see how dearly we should love God whenever some evil afflicts us, for by that one evil our most loving Father would want us to see how many evils would threaten and attack us if he himself did not stand in the way. It is as if he said, "Satan and a host of evils desire you that they may sift you as wheat [Luke 22:31], but I have been able to limit the sea and to say to it, 'To this place shall you come and here shall your proud waves be stayed,'" as he says in Job 38 [:11].

Were it to be that possibly none of these evils should come, if it so pleased God, nevertheless, death, known as the greatest of all terrors, is certain to come. Nothing is as uncertain as the hour of death's coming. Because death is such a great evil, we see many who would rather live with all the evils mentioned above than to die once and have them ended. Disdaining the other evils, this is the one to which the Scriptures ascribe fear, saying, "Remember your end, and then you will never sin" [Ecclus. 7:36]. Observe how many meditations, books, rules, and remedies have been amassed so that by calling the attention of men to this one evil, men might then fear sin, see the world as contemptible, lighten sufferings and evils, console the afflicted—all by a comparison with this great and terrible, yet so inevitable, evil of death. There is no one who would not choose to submit to all other evils if thereby he could avoid the evil of death. Even the saints dreaded it, and Christ submitted to it with trembling fear and bloody sweat [Luke 22:42-44]. Therefore, in no other area has divine mercy been more concerned about comforting faint hearts than in the matter of this evil, as we shall see below.

But just as all these evils are common to all men, so also are the blessings of salvation under these evils common to all. Christians have another and particular reason for dreading the evils to come, one which easily surpasses all evils previously mentioned. It is that which the Apostle depicts in I Corinthians 10 [:12] when he says, "Let him who stands take heed that he does not fall." The path is so very slippery and the foe is so very powerful, armed as he is with our own strength (that is, the aid given by our own flesh and all our evil desires), attended by the countless armies of the world, its pleasures and lusts on the right hand, its hardships and the evil intentions of men on the left. Besides all this, this foe is himself a master in the art of doing us harm, of reducing and destroying us in a thousand different ways.

Such is our life that not for a moment are we safe in our good intentions. Cyprian, who in his treatise *De Mortalitate* mentions many of these matters, teaches that death is to be wished for

129

as a quick means of escape from these evils.[10] And it is true that wherever there have been highminded men who gave deep thought to these infinite perils of hell, we see that in contempt of life and death (that is, of all the evils mentioned before), they desired to die and be delivered both from the evil of the sins in which they are now held (of which we spoke in connection with the previous image) and from the evil of the sins into which they are still able to fall (of which we are now speaking).

Indeed, these are two very weighty reasons we should not only seek death, but also disdain all evils, to say nothing of bearing lightly a single evil, as long as God grants us to be moved by them. It is God's gift if we are moved by them. What true Christian will not want death and even sickness when he sees that as long as he lives and is healthy, he is in sin and always likely to fall, yes, daily does fall into more sins, thus constantly thwarting the loving will of his loving Father? Paul was moved to such a heat of indignation in Romans 7 [:19, 24], when complaining that he did not do the good that he would but rather the evil that he would not, that he exclaimed, "Wretched man that I am. Who will deliver me from the body of this death?" The grace of God, he answers, through Jesus Christ, etc. [Rom. 7:25].

The man who does not prefer the evil of death to the evil of sin loves God his Father but little. God has ordained that this evil be brought to an end by death, and that death be the minister of life and righteousness. But more of this later.

Chapter Three: The Third Image

The Past Evil, or the Evil Behind Us

The sweet mercy of God the Father shines forth more brightly in this image than in the others and is able to comfort us in every distress. Never does a man feel the hand of God more closely upon him than when he remembers the years of his past life. St. Augustine says, "If a man were given the choice between dying and reliving his past life, he would surely choose death, seeing the great

---

[10] In *On Mortality.*

dangers and evils which he had so narrowly escaped."[11] When considered rightly, this statement is very true.

Here a man may see how often he has done and suffered many things without effort or care of his own, yes, even without or against his own will. He gave little thought to them before they occurred or while they were happening, and only after all was over did he find himself compelled to exclaim in great surprise, "How did these things happen to me, when I gave no thought to them, or thought something very different?" This bears out the proverb, "Man proposes, but God disposes" [Prov. 16:9]. That is, God turns things around and brings to pass something different from that which man had planned. Thus in this one respect alone it is not possible for us to deny that our lives and actions are under the guidance, not of our prudence, but of the wonderful power, wisdom, and goodness of God. Here we see how often God was with us when we neither saw nor sensed it, and how truthfully Peter has said, "He himself cares for us all" [I Pet. 5:7].

Therefore, even if there were no books or sermons, our very own lives, led through so many evils and dangers, would, if considered properly, abundantly commend to us the ever present and most tender goodness of God, which, far beyond our thought and feeling, carried us in its bosom. Thus Moses says in Deuteronomy 32 [:10], "The Lord kept him as the apple of his eye, and led him about, and carried him on his shoulders."

Out of this conviction the exhortations in the Psalter were born: "I remember the days of old; I meditate on all your works; I ponder the work of your hands" [Ps. 143:5]; "Surely I shall remember your wonders of old" [Ps. 77:11]; and, "I have remembered your judgments, and I am comforted" [Ps. 119:52]. These and other exhortations are all intended to teach us that since God was with us when we did not think so, or he did not seem to be with us, we should not doubt that he is always with us, even when it seems that he is absent from us. He who upheld us in many times of need, even without our request, will not forsake us in a smaller affliction, even though he seems to do so. Thus he says in Isaiah [54:7], "For a

---

[11] See his *Confessions*, xxix, 39.

brief moment I forsook you, but I will gather you with great mercies."

If you were to add to these passages the following: "Who cared for us during the many nights that we slept? Who cared for us while we worked, played, or were busy with those many activities in which we gave little thought to ourselves? Even the miser, eager in his quest for riches, finds it necessary to lay aside his care during his questing and dealing"—then we would see, whether we want to or not, that our entire care is completely in God's hand alone and that only rarely are we left to our own care. But now and then God permits even the latter to make us aware of his goodness that we might see the difference between his care and ours. Thus God now and then allows us to be assailed by some slight malady or other ill, as if hiding his care (though he never ceases to care), while, at the same time, he obstructs the many evils that would rush in upon us from all sides. He would then test us, his dearest children, to see whether we are willing to trust in his care which we knew before in life, and thus learn how vain and powerless our own care is. What benefit do we or can we bring to our entire life, when we are not able to heal a small pain in the leg[12] for even the shortest span of time?

Why, then, are we so anxious about a single peril or evil, instead of leaving the caring to him, when our whole life witnesses that he has rescued and delivered us from so many evils without any effort on our part? To know this, I say, is to know the works of God, to meditate on his works, and in our adversities to comfort ourselves by the remembrance of them [Ps. 143:5; 119:52]. Those who do not know this come up against the words in Psalm 28 [:5], "'Because they do not regard the works of God, or the works of his hand, you will destroy them and not build them up." They are ungrateful for all the care poured upon them by God during their lifetime and refuse even for a brief moment to commit their care to him.

---

[12] Luther may have had in mind the severe leg wound he suffered on the way home from Erfurt, probably on April 16, 1503. See Luther's recollection of the incident in LW 54, 14-15.

132

Chapter Four: The Fourth Image

The Infernal Evil, or the Evil Beneath Us

Until now we have seen in all the evils we endure only the divine goodness which is so great and so near to us that of all the countless evils which surround and tightly imprison us in this life, only a few—and even these not all the time—are permitted to assail us. Whenever we are oppressed by any present evil, therefore, it is to remind us of some great gain with which God honors us, insofar as he does not allow us to be overwhelmed by the multitude of evils surrounding us. Is it not a miracle to be struck only now and then by one of the countless blows aimed at us? It is indeed a blessing not to be struck by all. It is a miracle to be struck by but a few.

Of the evils beneath us the first is death and the other is hell.

When we consider the varied and terrible deaths by which other sinners are punished, we shall easily see how great our gain is in that we suffer less than we have deserved. How many men are hanged, strangled, drowned, or beheaded who perhaps committed sins much smaller than ours! Their deaths and misery are held up to us by Christ as an image by which we can see what we have deserved. In Luke 13 [:1-5] it is said that when they told him of the Galileans whose blood Pilate had mingled with their sacrifices, Christ answered, "Do you think that just because they suffered these things these Galileans were greater sinners than all the other Galileans? I say to you, No; but unless you repent, you shall all perish in like manner. Or do you think that the eighteen that were crushed and killed by the tower in Siloam were greater sinners than all the people who dwelt in Jerusalem? I say to you, No; but unless you repent, you shall all likewise perish." We who have committed the same or even graver sins cannot expect to escape with a lighter punishment. Nor will the justice and truth of God, ordained to render to every man according to his deeds [Rom. 2:6], be turned into injustice and a lie just for our sake, unless we hasten to make amends by at least bearing our minor evil with patience.

And as for hell and everlasting damnation, how many thousands are there who have not committed the thousandth part of our sins! How many virgins, youths, and those whom we call in-

133

nocents are there! How many monks, priests, and married couples! All their lives they seemed to be serving God, and now, perhaps because of a single lapse, they are being punished forever. It must not be denied that God's justice is the same in the case of every sin, hating and punishing it in whomever it is found. Do we not see here the inestimable mercy of God, who has not condemned us though we fully deserved it? I ask you, what are all the sufferings life can bring compared with the eternal punishment which they indeed suffer justly because of one sin, while we go free and unpunished for our many sins which God has covered? [Ps. 32:1]. That we give no thought to these benefits of God or esteem them only lightly is a sign of our ingratitude and a hardening of our unbelieving and unfeeling hearts.

Furthermore, we must include here the many infidels, heathen, Jews, and children, who, if they had been favored with the advantages given to us, would not now be in hell, but in heaven, and would have sinned far less than we. Christ sets this mirror before our eyes when he says in Matthew [11:21-24], "Woe to you, Chorazin! Woe to you, Bethsaida! If the mighty works which were done in you had been done in Tyre and Sidon, they would have repented long ago in sackcloth and ashes. But I say to you, nevertheless, that on the day of judgment it will be more tolerable for Tyre and Sidon than for you. And you, Capernaum, that was exalted into heaven, you shall be brought down into hell, for if the mighty deeds which were done in you had been done in Sodom, it would have remained to this day. But I say to you that it shall be more tolerable in the day of judgment for Sodom than for you."

We see, therefore, how much praise and love we owe our gracious God in every evil of this life, for each is scarcely a drop of the evils which we have deserved and which Job compares to the sea and to the sand on the shore [Job 6:3].

Chapter Five: The Fifth Image

The Evil on Our Left Hand

Here we must hold before our eyes the vast multitude of adversaries and wicked men. We must consider, first, how many evils they would have inflicted on our bodies, property, good name, and soul, but were unable to because of the providence of God. The higher a man's position in life and the broader his rule,[13] the more he is exposed to such persecution, intrigues, slander, and plots of his enemies. In all this we may again mark and feel the nearness of God's hand. Should we be surprised if now and then we are touched by one of these evils?

Again, we should take note of the evils which these men themselves endure—not to exult over them, but that we may feel pity for them. In common with us, they are exposed to all the same evils, which can be seen easily in the preceding images. However, their plight is worse than ours, because in a both bodily and spiritual sense they are outside of our fellowship.[14] The evil that we endure is nothing compared to their estate, for they are in sin and unbelief, under the wrath of God and under the dominion of the devil, wretched slaves to ungodliness and sin. Even if the whole world were to heap curses on them, it could not wish them anything worse than what they have.

If we consider this rightly, we shall see how greatly we are favored by God in that we may bear some slight bodily ill while in the faith, in the kingdom of Christ, and in the service of God. We ought not even to feel it, since we are in the midst of such rich blessings. Yes, this misery of theirs should so disturb a Christian's pious heart that his own troubles seem like pleasures. Thus St. Paul exhorts in Philippians 2 [:4-7], "Let each man give thought to the things of others, and not only to his own. Let this mind be in you, which was also in Christ Jesus, who, though he might be in the form of God, accepted the form of a servant, etc." That is to say, he took our form upon himself and lived in the midst of our evils no differently than if they were his own, forgetting himself and emptying himself of all his goods, so that he was found to be utterly in the likeness of man, counting nothing human as alien to himself and giving himself wholly over to our evils.

Inspired by this love and moved by this example, the saints are wont to pray for wicked men, even for their enemies, and, fur-

---

[13] This is another specific allusion to the Elector.
[14] I.e., the fellowship or communion of saints.

ther, to do all things after the example of Christ while forgetting their own injuries and rights, to think only of how they might rescue them from their evils, which torment them more cruelly than their own bodily evils. Thus St. Peter writes in II Peter 2 [:8] about Lot, "He dwelt among them who day after day tormented his just soul with evil deeds."

You see how deep is the abyss of evils that is here opened up, and how it is an opportunity for pity and compassion and for over-looking our own paltry ills, if the love of God abides in us. What God permits us to suffer is nothing compared to what they suffer. The reason these things affect us so little is that our hearts are not able to see how great is the shame and misery of a man lying in sin, that is, separated from God and possessed of the devil. Who is so hard of heart as not to sicken at the wretched sight of those lying at the doors of the churches and in the streets, with disfigured faces, their noses, eyes, and other members so hideously consumed with festering sores that the mind is terrified and the senses recoil from the sight?[15] What else does God intend with these lamentable specimens of our flesh and friendship but to enable us to see in our mind's eye even more horrible forms in which the sinner's soul shows forth its disease and decay, even though he himself may live in purple and gold among roses and lilies like a child of paradise? Yet how many sinners are there in the world to each one of those wretched creatures! When we disregard those evils of our neigh-bors, great in both number and degree, it follows that our own evil, though it be but the most trivial, will appear to us to be the only one and the greatest of all.

But there is more! Even in regard to bodily ills, these people are worse off than we are. How can they, I ask you, find sweet and pure joys, even if they have obtained everything their heart desires, as long as their conscience can find no peace? Can there be an evil more dreadful than the unrest of a gnawing conscience? In Isaiah 57 [:20-21] we read, "The wicked are like the troubled sea when it cannot rest, whose waves cast up mire and dirt. There is no peace for the wicked, says the Lord God." You may see the same

---

[15] Luther alludes to the beggars and other unfortunates (as well as rascals) who loitered before the churches in the hope of receiving alms.

136

thing in Deuteronomy 28 [:65-67], "The Lord shall give you a trembling heart, failing eyes, and a sorrowful mind. Your life shall hang in doubt before you. You shall be in fear day and night, and shall not have faith in your life. In the morning you will say, 'Would that it were evening,' and in the evening you will say, 'Would that it were morning,' because of the fear in your heart which terrifies you, and because of what you see with your eyes."

In brief, when all the evils of the wicked are viewed in the right spirit, whether they belong to enemies or friends, a man will then not only forget his own evil, but it will seem to him as if he were not suffering at all. With Moses [Exod. 32:32] and the Apostle Paul, he would desire to die for them, to be separated from Christ and expunged from the book of life, as is written in Romans 9 [:3], just so that they might be set free. Christ was enkindled with such zeal and fervor when he died for us and descended into hell [I Pet. 3:19], leaving us an example that we should be concerned with the evils of others and completely forgetful of our own—no, covetous of our own.

Chapter Six: The Sixth Image

The Evil on Our Right Hand

On the right hand are our friends, whose evil makes our own lighter, as St. Peter teaches in I Peter 5 [:9], saying, "Resist the devil in firm faith, knowing that the same sufferings are inflicted on your brethren in the world." The church in its prayers also petitions that, urged on by the example of the saints, we might imitate the virtue of their sufferings. The church sings:

What torments all the saints endured,

That they might win the martyr's palm![16]

From such words and hymns of the church we learn that the feasts of the saints, their memorials, churches, altars, names, and pictures are observed and multiplied to inspire others by their example to bear the same evils which they also bore. Unless they are observed in this light, the cult of the saints cannot be free of superstition.

---

[16] The passage is an antiphon in the widely used Roman breviary. *BG* 6, 25, n. 1.

There are many who observe all these things only to escape the very evil which the saints, by their example and memory, teach us should be borne. They thus become unlike those whose feasts they celebrate to become like them.

The finest treatment of this section of our *Consolations* is given by the Apostle, when he says in Hebrews 12 [:4-11], "Until now you have not resisted to the point of bleeding in your struggle against sin. You have forgotten the exhortation in which you were addressed as sons: 'My son, do not take lightly the chastening of the Lord, nor become weary when you are rebuked by him. The Lord loves him whom he chastens, and he scourges every son whom he receives.' Endure your chastening, for in it God is treating you as sons. What son is there whom his father does not discipline? If you are left without the chastening in which all others share, you are bastards and not sons. Moreover, we have had fathers in the flesh who chastened us and we showed them respect. Shall we not subject ourselves even more to the Father of spirits, and thus live? All chastisement seems at the moment to be not for our pleasure but to our sorrow, but hereafter it offers the peaceful fruit of righteousness to those who have been exercised by it."

This is what Paul says. Who would not be terrified by these words of Paul in which he clearly states that those who are without the chastisement of God are not then children of God? On the other hand, who could be more powerfully enheartened and more fully comforted than he who hears that those who are chastened are loved by the Lord, that they are sons of God, that they are members in the communion of saints, and that those who suffer are never alone? Such a powerful exhortation must make chastisement something to be loved.

There is no room here for the excuse that some have lighter and others heavier burdens to bear. To everyone is given temptation according to a measure and never beyond his strength. It is written in Psalm 80 [:5], "You shall feed us with the bread of tears, and for our drink give us tears in full measure." Paul says, "God is faithful, and he will not let you be tempted beyond your strength, but with the temptation will also make a way of escape, so that you may be able to bear it" [I Cor. 10:13]. Therefore, where there is greater evil, there is also more divine help and a way of escape, so that the inequality of suffering appears to be greater than it really is.

Does not St. John the Baptist, whose beheading by Herod we commemorate today,[17] shame and amaze us all? We must be amazed that so great a man—no greater was born of woman [Matt. 11:11]—the special friend of the bridegroom [John 3:29], the forerunner of Christ, greater than all the prophets [Matt. 11:9], should have been put to death, not after a public trial, not on a false charge (as in the case of Christ), not for the sake of the people. No, he perished in a dungeon, for the sake of a dancing girl, the daughter of an adulteress! The ignominious death of this one saint, as well as the vile and shameless surrender of his life into the hands of the vengeful adulteress, should make every one of our evils light. Where was God, that he could look at such things? Where was Christ, who heard it and was completely silent [Matt. 14:13]? This man died as if unknown to God, man, and all creatures. Compared with such a death, what sufferings have we to boast of? Rather, what sufferings have we which we should not be ashamed of? In what light will we appear with our unwillingness to suffer, next to this man who endured such a shameful and undeserved death, and whose body was insulted by his enemies after his death? "Look," he says in Jeremiah [49:12], "if those whose judgment was not to drink the cup did drink it, will you then be free to go unpunished? You shall not go unpunished, but shall surely drink of it."

That was why that hermit who was ill year after year rightly wept and lamented when he was in sound health for a whole year, assuming it was because God had forsaken him and denied him his grace.[18] So necessary and so salutary is the Lord's chastening for all Christians.

We thus see that all our suffering is nothing when we consider the nails, dungeons, irons, faggots, wild beasts, and countless tortures of the saints, and also when we ponder the afflictions of men

---

[17] The beheading of John the Baptist [Matt. 14:1-12] was observed on August 29. PE 1, 134, n. 2. The passage helps to date this writing.
[18] Luther probably alludes to Jerome's Lives of the Hermits.

now living, who in our lifetime endure the most grievous persecutions of the devil. There is no lack of men who suffer more intensely and more bitterly both in body and soul than we do.

But some may say, "It is my complaint that my sufferings cannot be compared with the sufferings of the saints. I am a sinner and do not deserve to be compared with them. They suffered for their innocence, but I suffer for my sins. Little wonder that they bore everything so blithely!" That is a very stupid statement. If you suffer because of your sins, then you ought to rejoice that you are being purged of your sins. Then, too, were not the saints also sinners? Do you fear that you are like Herod or the thief on Christ's left hand [Luke 23:39-43]? You are not, if you have patience. How did the thief on the left hand differ from the one on the right except in the patience of the one and the impatience of the other? If you are a sinner, good! The thief was also a sinner, but by his patience he merited[19] the glory of righteousness and holiness. Go and do likewise [Luke 10:37]. Whenever you suffer, it is either because of your sins or your righteousness. Both kinds of suffering sanctify and save if you will but love them. Thus there is no excuse that remains.

Finally, as soon as you have confessed that you suffer deservedly for your sins, you are as righteous and holy as the thief on the right hand. Since confession of sins is truth, it justifies and sanctifies. Thus in the very moment of your confession, you are no longer suffering for your sins, but for your innocence. The righteous man always suffers innocently. You are made righteous by the confession of your deserved suffering and sins. Thus your suffering may be compared with the sufferings of the saints as truly and worthily as your confession of sins may be compared with the confession of the saints. There is only one truth in the midst of everything, only one confession of all sins, one suffering of all evils, and one true communion of saints in all and through all.

---

[19] Here Luther employs the terminology of Roman Catholic theology (*BG* 6, 28, n. 1). By allowing this and similar passages to stand unaltered in published versions, Luther gave his opponents material for their collection of contradictions culled from his writings. For an example of such efforts by his foes, see *LW* 46, 82-83.

Chapter Seven: The Seventh Image
The Supernal Evil, or the Evil Above Us

Finally, let us lift up our hearts[20] and ascend with the bride into the mountain of myrrh [Song of Sol. 4:6]. Here is Jesus Christ, the Crucified, head of all the saints, the prince of all sufferers, of whom many have written much and all have written everything,[21] as is fitting. His memory is commended to the bride when it is said, "Set me as a seal upon your heart and as a seal upon your arm" [Song of Sol. 8:6]. The blood of the lamb, stained across the threshold, wards off the destructive angel [Exod. 12:13]. The bride is praised by him because the hair of her head is like the king's purple [Song of Sol. 7:5], that is, she glows red as she recalls and meditates on the passion of Christ. This is the tree which Moses was commanded to cast into the waters of Marah—which means the bitterness of suffering—and they were made sweet [Exod. 15:23-25].

There is nothing, not even death, that his passion cannot sweeten. Thus the bride says, "His lips are lilies, letting sweet-smelling myrrh fall in drops" [Song of Sol. 5:13]. What resemblance is there between lilies and lips, since lips are red and lilies white? It is said in a mystical sense, as if to say that Christ's words are clear and pure, without even a vestige of bloodred bitterness or malice, but only sweetness and mildness. Yet into them he drops precious and chosen myrrh (that is, the most bitter death). These purest and sweetest lips have the power to make the bitterest death sweet and fair and bright and dear, for death (like precious myrrh) removes all of sin's corruptions at once.

How does this come to pass? Surely, it comes to pass when you hear that Jesus Christ, God's Son, has by his most holy touch consecrated and hallowed all sufferings, even death itself, has blessed the curse, and has glorified shame and enriched poverty so that death is now a door to life, the curse a fount of blessing, and shame the mother of glory. How, then, can you be so hardhearted and ungrateful as not to long for and love all manner of sufferings now that these have been touched and bathed by Christ's pure and holy

---

[20] The expression echoes the language of the *Sursum Corda* in the Preface of the mass.

[21] The "many" and "all" probably mean the biblical authors.

141

flesh and blood and thus have become holy, harmless, wholesome, blessed, and full of joy for you?

For if Christ by the touch of his most innocent flesh has hallowed all waters, yes, even all creation, through baptism, how much more has he by the same touch of his most innocent flesh and blood sanctified every form of death, all suffering and loss, every curse and shame for the baptism of the Spirit, or the baptism of blood![22] Of this baptism of suffering he says in Luke 12 [:50], "I have a baptism to be baptized with, and how I am constrained until it is accomplished!" Here you see how he is constrained, how he pants and thirsts to sanctify sufferings and death and to make them things to be loved, for he saw how we stand in fear of sufferings, how we tremble and shrink from death. Therefore, as a godly pastor and faithful physician, he hastens to set limits to this our evil, and is impatient to die and by his touch to commend suffering and evil to us. Thus the death of a Christian is now to be regarded as the bronze serpent of Moses [Num. 21:8-9], which in all respects has the appearance of a serpent, yet is completely without life, motion, venom, and sting. Though in the eyes of the unwise the righteous seem to die, they are at peace [Wisd. of Sol. 3:2-3]. In death we are like all other men: the outward mode of our dying is not unlike that of others, except the thing itself is different, since for us death is dead. In like manner, all our sufferings are like the sufferings of others, but only in appearance. In reality, our sufferings are the beginning of our freedom as our death is the beginning of life. It is this which Christ says in John 8 [:51], "Whoever will keep my word shall never see death." How shall he not see it? Because in his death he enters upon life, so that because of the life that he sees he is not able to see death. Here the night shines as the day [Ps. 139:12], since the dawning life is brighter than the waning death. This is assured not for the unbelievers, but for all

---

[22] Luther alludes here to the three kinds of baptism: by water, i.e., sacramentally administered; by fire, i.e., by the Spirit, apart from sacramental administration; and by blood, i.e., the shedding of blood in martyrdom. Cf. *PE* 1, 138, n. 1.

[23] Elector Frederick was noted for his extensive collection of relics, housed in the Church of All Saints in Wittenberg. A catalog of the collection published in 1509 listed 5,005 items, including a fragment of the crown of thorns and

who believe in Christ.

If you kiss, caress, and embrace as sweetest relics[23] the robe of Christ,[24] the vessels, the water jugs, and anything Christ touched or used or hallowed by his touch, why will you not much more rather love, embrace, and kiss the pain and evils of this world, the disgrace and shame which he not only hallowed by his touch but sprinkled and blessed with his most holy blood, yes, even embraced with a willing heart and with supreme, constraining love? The more so, since for you there are far greater merits, rewards, and blessings in these sufferings than in those relics. In them victory over death, hell, and all sins is offered to you, but in those relics nothing at all.

Oh, if we could only see the heart of Christ as he was suspended from the cross, anguishing to make death contemptible and dead for us. How fervently and cheerfully he embraced death and pain for us timid souls who are horrified by death and pain! How willingly he first drank this cup for us sick ones, so that we might not shrink from drinking it after him! In his resurrection we see that nothing evil befell him, in fact, only the greatest good. If we could see this, then undoubtedly that precious myrrh dropping from Christ's lips and commended by his words would be sweet and appealing to us, even as the fragrance and beauty of the lilies. Thus St. Peter says in I Peter 4 [:1], "Since Christ suffered in the flesh, arm yourselves with that thought." St. Paul says in Hebrews 12 [:3], "Consider him who endured such hostility from sinners against himself, so that you may not be weary or fainthearted."

If we have learned from the preceding images, those beneath and near us, to bear our evils with patience, then surely this last image, in which we are lifted above and outside ourselves, caught

---

some of Mary's milk. By 1520 the collection included 19,013 items. The veneration of these relics on All Saints' Day (November 1) could win indulgences totaling more than five hundred thousand years. *PE* 1, 139, n. 1, and *The New Schaff-Herzog Encyclopedia of Religious Knowledge,* ed. Samuel Macauley Jackson (New York: Funk and Wagnalls, 1912), IV, 376. On the possible relationship between this collection of relics and Luther's posting of the *Ninety-five Theses* on the eve of All Saints' Day, 1517, see *PE* 1, 15-16.

[24] A relic regarded as the garment worn by Christ on the cross (John 19:23-24) had, according to legend, been given to the cathedral at Trier by the mother of Constantine the Great. *PE* 2, 130, n. 1.

up into Christ and placed beyond all evils, should teach us that we ought not only to tolerate these evils, but love them, desire them, and seek them out. If such thinking is still foreign to a person, it means that the passion of Christ still has little meaning for him. This is evident in those who make the signs and arms of Christ to ward off evils and death,[25] but are not ready to suffer or to die. This is altogether contrary to the cross and death of Christ.

In keeping with this image we must therefore absorb and consume whatever evils we may have to bear, so that they will not only not grieve us, but will delight us. This will come true if this image finds its way into our heart and abides in the innermost affections of our mind. This is the first panel. The second follows.

The second part also consists of seven images, the opposite of the seven in the first part. Of these, the first represents the internal blessing; the second, the future blessing; the third, the past blessing; the fourth, the infernal blessing; the fifth, the blessing on the left hand; the sixth, the blessing on the right hand; and the seventh, the supernal blessing.

The First Chapter: The First Image

The Blessing Within Us

What person is there who can count up even only those blessings he has within himself? How great, first of all, are the gifts of the body! Beauty, strength, health, and the alertness of the senses! In the case of the male, there is also the greater nobility of his sex, which enables him to do many things both in public and private life, as well as many splendid achievements to which woman is a stranger. And if, by the grace of God, you enjoy the use of these excellent gifts for ten, twenty, or thirty years, and in that time suffer for a few days now and then, how bad is that? There is a saying current among scoundrels which says, "It is merely a matter of one bad hour." And another one is, "One good hour makes up for a bad one." What then is to be done about us, who have received so many good hours and are not willing to endure evil for one hour. So we see how many blessings God showers upon us and

---

[25] I.e., to bless oneself with the sign of the cross.

how few evils barely touch us. That is true at least for most of us.

But not content with these blessings, our gracious God adds riches and an abundance of things, if not to all, certainly to many and especially to those who are too weak to bear evils. For, as I said before, when he grants fewer bodily gifts to someone, he gives greater gifts of the mind, so that all things will be equal and he will be the just judge of all. Great wealth is not as comforting as a cheerful mind. Moreover, to some God also grants children, the greatest (it is said) pleasure, influence, rank, honor, fame, glory, favor, and the like. The enjoyment of these for a long or even a short season will soon teach us how we ought to conduct ourselves in the face of some small evil.

But more excellent than all these are the blessings of the mind, such as, reason, judgment, knowledge, eloquence, and prudence. In these, as in other instances, God tempers the justice of his dealings, so that when he confers more of these gifts on some, he does not prefer these to the others, on whom he confers a greater peace and cheerfulness of mind. In all these matters we should gratefully acknowledge the bountiful hand of God and should take comfort in our infirmity. We should not be surprised if among so many and great blessings there is some intermingling of bitterness. Even for epicures no meat is savory without salt, nor is scarcely any dish palatable that does not have a certain bitter taste, either native or produced by seasoning. So intolerable is constant and unvarying sweetness that it has truly been said, "Every pleasure too long continued turns into loathing" and also, "Even pleasure itself turns into suffering." Because of the excessive abundance of good things, we are unable to enjoy only good things in this life without a tempering of evil. This has given rise to the saying, "One must have strong bones to bear the good days." Whenever I pondered this saying I always admired it for its excellent true sense, namely, that the wishes of men always conflict with each other, so that when the good days arrive which they desired, they are less able to bear them than the evil days.

What, then, is it that God would have us lay to heart, except that the cross is held in honor even among the enemies of the cross? Is there anything that must not be tempered and sanctified with the relics of the cross to prevent decay, just as meat must be seasoned with salt lest it breed maggots? Why then do we not gladly accept this tempering sent by God, which, if he were not to send it, our own life, weakened by pleasures and blessings, would demand of itself? Thus we see how truthfully the Book of Wisdom says of God, "He reaches mightily from end to end and orders all things well" [Wisd. of Sol. 8:1]. When we examine these blessings, the truth of Moses' words in Deuteronomy 32 [:10] will be clear, "He bore him on his shoulders, he led him around, and guarded him like the apple of his eye." With these words we can stop the mouths of those ungrateful babblers who say that in this life there is more evil than good. There is no lack of blessings and there are countless sweet blessings, but there is a scarcity of those who have the same insight as he who said, "The earth is full of the mercy of the Lord" [Ps. 33:5], and again, "The earth is full of his praise" [Hab. 3:3], and again, in Psalm 104 [:24], "The earth is full of your riches"; "O Lord, you have made me glad by your work" [Ps. 92:4].

Daily in the mass we sing, "Heaven and earth are full of your glory" [Isa. 6:3].[26] Why do we sing this? Because of the many blessings for which God must be praised, although this is done only by those who see the fulness of them. As we said concerning the evils of the first image, a man's evils are only as great as his knowledge and opinion of them; so it is with his blessings. Though they rush in and crowd upon us from every side, they are only as great as we acknowledge them to be. All things that God does are exceedingly good [Gen. 1:31], but they are not acknowledged as good by all, for example, by those of whom it is said in Psalm 106 [:24], "They despised the pleasant land."

The most beautiful and instructive example of this image is furnished by Job [2:10], who after the loss of his possessions said, "If we receive good from the hand of God, why should we not also bear evil?" Truly, that is a golden saying and a great comfort in the day of trial. Not only did Job suffer, but he was also tempted to impatience by his wife when she said to him, "Do you still maintain your uprightness? Curse God, and die" [Job 2:9]. It was as if she said, "It is plain that he who forsakes you is not God. Why,

---

[26] The passage is sung in the Sanctus of the mass.

then, do you trust in him? Why not renounce and curse him instead, and acknowledge that you are a mortal for whom there is nothing after this life?" Thoughts like these are suggested to each person by his wife (that is, by his carnal mind) in time of temptation, for the carnal mind does not savor things that are of God.[27]

However, these bodily blessings are common to all. But a Christian has other and far better blessings within, namely, faith in Christ, of which it is said in Psalm 45 [:13], "The king's daughter is all glorious within; her clothing is of wrought gold." Just as we asserted of the evil in the first image, that no matter how great the evil in man, it is not the worst possible for him, so we say now that the Christian is unable to see the greatest blessings within himself. If he could perceive them, he would be in heaven at once, since the kingdom of heaven (as Christ says) is within us [Luke 17:21]. To have faith is to have the Word and truth of God, and to have the Word of God is to have God himself, the maker of all. If all these blessings in their fulness were revealed to the soul, it would in a moment break free from the body because of its exceeding abundance of sweet pleasure. Therefore, all the other blessings of which we have spoken are but monitors of the blessings which we have within us and which God would commend to us by them. Since this life of ours cannot bear to have them revealed, God mercifully keeps them hidden until they have reached their full measure. It is like loving parents who at times give their children foolish little toys with which they would lead their hearts to hope for better things.

At times, nevertheless, these inner blessings show themselves and break out, as when a person with a happy conscience rejoices in his trust in God, speaks openly about him, hears his Word with eagerness, and is ready and quick to serve him and do good works, to suffer evil, etc. These are all signs of the infinite and incomparable blessings hidden within, which like a small spring, send forth little drops and tiny rills. Sometimes it is revealed more fully to contemplative souls, who, in their rapture, no longer know where they are. Such experiences are related by St. Augustine and his mother,[28] as well as by many others.

---

[27] Cf. Matt. 16:23.
[28] *Confessions,* ix, 10.

Chapter Two: The Second Image

The Future Blessing or the Blessing Before Us

While in the midst of their evils, those who are not Christians will find but little comfort in contemplating future blessings, since for them all things are uncertain. Although we make much ado about that famous emotion called hope, calling on each other in human comfort to hope for better times, we are still always deceived. It is the same thing that Christ shows us in the case of the man in the Gospel of Luke, chapter 12 [:16-21], who said to his soul, " 'I will pull down my barns, and build greater. And I will say to my soul: My soul, take your ease, eat, drink, and be merry. You have ample goods laid up for many years.' But God said to him, 'O fool, this night they will require your soul of you. To whom, then, will those things belong that you have prepared?' So is he who lays up treasures and is not rich toward God."

Yet God has not forsaken the sons of men, but comforts them with the hope that the evils will pass and that good things shall come. Though they must remain uncertain about the future, they yet hope with a sure hope which sustains them in the meanwhile, lest falling into despair they are unable to bear up under the present evil and do something that is worse.[29] Hence, even this kind of hope is the gift of God. He does not want man to lean on it, but rather to see it as a reminder of the firm hope which is in God alone. He is patient enough with them to lead them to repentance, as Romans 2 [:4] says. He steadfastly allows no one to be deceived by this deceitful hope, if they will but "return to the heart" [Isa. 46:8] and come to the true hope.

In addition to this twofold blessing, Christians certainly have the greatest blessings of all awaiting them in the future. However, these are attained only through sufferings and death. They surely also rejoice in that common and uncertain hope that the evil of the present will come to an end and that its opposite, the blessing, will increase, but this is not their chief concern. Their chief concern is that their own particular blessing might increase, namely, the

---

[29] The "something worse" is suicide.

truth that is in Christ, in which they advance day by day and for which they live and hope. But besides this blessing they have, as I have said, the two greatest blessings in their death. The first is that through death the whole tragedy of this world's ills is ended. Thus it is written, "Precious in the sight of the Lord is the death of his saints" [Ps. 116:15], and, "In peace shall I lie down and sleep" [Ps. 4:8], and, "Though the righteous man be seized by death, he shall be at rest" [Wisd. of Sol. 4:7]. But for the ungodly, on the other hand, death is the beginning of evils, as it is written, "The death of sinners is most evil" [Ps. 34:21], and also, "Evils shall seize the unjust man unto destruction" [Ps. 140:11]. Thus Lazarus, who received his evils in his lifetime, will be comforted, while the rich glutton will be tormented because he received his good things here [Luke 16:25].

Whether he lives or dies, the Christian is thus always in a better state. How blessed it is to be a Christian and to believe in Christ! That is why Paul says, "For me to live is Christ, and to die is gain" [Phil. 1:21]. In Romans 14 [:8] he says, "If a man lives, he lives unto the Lord; if he dies, he dies unto the Lord. Whether we live, therefore, or die, we are the Lord's." This security Christ has won for us by his death and resurrection, so that he might be the Lord of both the living and the dead, and be able to keep us as safe in death as in life. Thus Psalm 23 [:4] says, "Though I walk through the valley of the shadow of death, I will fear no evil, because you are with me." If this gain through death has only a small affect on us, it is proof that our faith in Christ is still feeble and does not prize highly enough the reward and gain of a blessed death, nor does it yet believe that death is a blessing. Obviously, we are hindered because the old man and the wisdom of the flesh are still too much alive in us. We should, therefore, try to attain to the knowledge and the love of this blessing of death. It is a great thing that death, which to others is the greatest of evils, is made the greatest gain for us. If it was not this that Christ obtained for us, what then did he do that was worth such a cost, yes, actually the cost of his life? It is indeed a divine work that he wrought, and it is not surprising that he made the evil of death into the greatest blessing.

149

For the believer death is thus already dead and behind its cloak and mask it holds no terrors. Like a slain serpent, death still has its former terrifying appearance, but now this is only a mask, for it is now a dead and harmless evil. Just as in Numbers 21 [:8-9] God commanded Moses to raise up a brass serpent, at the sight of which the living serpents perished, so also does our death die when our eyes of faith rest upon the death of Christ. It is only the outward appearance of death that remains. By means of such splendid symbols the mercy of God shows us in our infirmity that even though death should not be taken away, its power has been reduced by him to a mere shadow. This is the reason that in the Scriptures it is called a sleep rather than death.[30]

The other blessing of death is that death not only puts an end to the evils of this life's punishments, but that death also—which is even more excellent—puts an end to all sins and vices. As we have said above, this renders death far more desirable for believing souls than the former blessing, since the evils of the soul, namely, its sins, are incomparably worse than the evils of the body. If we but realized it, this alone should make death very desirable. If it does not do that, it is a sign that we neither feel nor hate the sins of our soul as we should. With slippery sin besetting us on all sides, our life is so full of perils that we are unable to live without sinning. Thus death is indeed the greatest blessing as it delivers us from these perils and cuts sin fully away from us. In praise of the just man the Wisdom of Solomon [4:10-14] concludes, "The man pleasing to God was loved by him and while living among sinners was taken up. He was caught up lest wickedness change his understanding or guile deceive his soul. For the fascination of naughtiness obscures what is good, and the erring desire perverts the innocent mind. (Oh, how true this always is!) Being perfected in a short time, he now lived a long time. Because his soul was pleasing to the Lord, he hastened to lead him away from the wicked."

Thus (by the mercy of God) death, which for man was the punishment for his sin, has for the Christian been made the end of sin and the beginning of life and righteousness. Therefore, he

---

[30] Cf. Matt. 9:24; I Thess. 4:13.

who loves life and righteousness must not hate, but rather love, death, his servant and workshop, if he desires to attain to either life or righteousness. Let him who is not able to do this, pray God to enable him to do it. To this end we are taught to pray, "Thy will be done," because we cannot do this ourselves, since in our fear of death we love death and sin rather than life and righteousness. And that God appointed death to be the destroyer of death can be gathered from the fact that he imposed death on Adam immediately after his sin as a cure for sin [Gen. 3:19]. God did this before he drove him out of paradise to show us that death works us no evil but rather every blessing, since it was imposed in paradise as a penance and satisfaction. It is true that through the envy of the devil death entered into the world, but it is evidence of God's surpassing goodness that after death entered, it is not permitted to harm us, but is taken captive from the very beginning and appointed to be the punishment and death of sin.

This God indicated when, having warned Adam of his death in this precept, he afterward did not remain silent, but imposed death once more, though tempering the hardness of his commandment. Not even mentioning death with a single syllable, he said only, "You are dust and to dust you shall return," and, "Until you return to the ground from which you were taken" [Gen. 3:19]. It was as if even God hated death so bitterly that he did not deem it worthy to call it by name, in accordance with the word, "Wrath is in his indignation and life in his good will" [Ps. 30:5]. Thus he seemed to say that unless death had been necessary to abolish sin, he would not have wanted to know it or name it, much less to impose it. Thus the zeal of God arms this very death against the sin which had caused death, so that you may see the truth spoken by the poet, "The artist perishes by his own art." [31] So also, sin is destroyed by its own fruit and is slain by the death to which it gave birth, as a viper is devoured by its own offspring. It is a glorious spectacle to see how sin is destroyed, not by the work of another, but by its own, and how it is stabbed with its own sword, as Goliath is beheaded by his own sword [I Sam. 17:51]. Goliath also was a kind of sin, a giant terrifying to all except the young

---

[31] Ovid, *The Art of Love*, i, 656.

151

boy David, that is, to Christ, who singlehandedly laid him low, beheaded him with his own sword, and in I Samuel 21 [:9] said that there was no better sword than the sword of Goliath.

Therefore, if we meditate on these joys of the power of Christ and on the gifts of his grace, how can any small evil distress us when in the great evil that is to come we see such a great blessing?

Chapter Three: The Third Image

The Past Blessings, or the Blessings Behind Us

The consideration of this image is easy since it is made in contrast to the evils of the past. We shall, however, help him who makes such a comparison. Here St. Augustine is an excellent master in his *Confessions,* in which he recites so beautifully the benefits of God toward him from his mother's womb.[32] The same is done in Psalm 139 [:1-3], "Lord, you have searched me," in which the psalmist, marveling among other things at the goodness of God, says, "You have understood my thoughts from afar, you have known my path and my lying down." It is as though he said, "I see now that whatever I have ever thought or done, whatever I shall attain or possess, will not be the result of my labors, but because long ago it was ordered by your solicitude for me, since you have foreknown all my ways. In my tongue there is no speech. Where, then, is it? In your power!"

We learn this from our own experience. When we reflect on our past life, is it not amazing that we thought, desired, did, and said things that we were not able to foresee? How very different our course would have been if we had been left to our own free will! Only now do we understand God's ever-present care and providence over us, so that we were able neither to think nor speak anything except as he gave us leave. Thus it is written in the Wisdom of Solomon 7 [:16], "In his hands are both we and our words," and by Paul, "Who works all things in me" [I Cor. 12:6]. Should not we, calloused and hard of heart, hang our heads in shame when we learn from our own experience how the Lord has cared for us

---

[32] *Confessions,* i, 6.

to this present hour and given us every blessing? Yet we cannot commit our care to him in even a small present evil, and we act as if he had forsaken us or could forsake us! This is not the position of Psalm 40 [:17], "I am poor and needy, but the Lord takes thought of me." St. Augustine says this, "Let him who made you care for you. Why should he who cared for you before you existed not care for you now that you are what he willed you to be?" [33] However, we seek to divide the governing between God and ourselves. Reluctantly we concede that he made us, but to ourselves we arrogate the care over ourselves. We act as if after God made us, he departed at once and left the governing of ourselves in our own hands.

But if our own wisdom and judgment blind us to the providence of God in our lives, just because by some chance many things developed in accordance with our own plans, let us once again search into our lives and say with Psalm 139 [:15-16], "My frame was not hidden from you when I was made in secret (that is, you fashioned and beheld my bones in my mother's womb, when as yet I was not, and my mother did not know what was forming in her), and my substance was fashioned in the lowest parts of the earth (that is, even the form and figure of my body in the secret chambers of the womb were not hidden from you, for you were fashioning it)." What else does the psalmist intend with such words except to show us by this marvelous illustration how God has always cared for us without any help from us! Who can boast of having had a part in his formation in the womb? Who gave to our mothers the concern to suckle, fondle, and love us, and to perform all the duties of motherhood before we were even conscious of our life? Would we know or remember any of these things unless, having observed the same things done to others, we now believe that they were done to us also? As far as our knowledge of them is concerned, they were performed for us when we were still in a sleep, no, rather dead, or really not yet born.

Thus we see how without all our doing divine compassion and comfort sustain us. Still we doubt, even despair, that he cares for us today. If this experience does not instruct and move us, I do not know what will. All this is demonstrated to us in every infant.

---

[33] *Commentary on Psalm 39* [40] *(Commentatio in psalmum XXXIX)*, 17.

So many examples offered to our foolishness and hardness of heart ought well to fill us with deep shame, if we ever doubt that the slightest blessing or evil can come to us without the particular providence of God. Thus St. Peter says in I Peter 5 [:7], "Cast all your cares upon him because he cares for you." Psalm 55 [:22] says, "Cast your burden on the Lord and he will sustain you." In his *Confessions* St. Augustine addresses his soul in this manner, "Why do you stand upon yourself and yet do not stand? Cast yourself on him. He will not withdraw his hand and let you fall." [34] And again we read in I Peter 4 [:19], "Therefore, let those who suffer according to the will of God commit their souls to the faithful Creator in well doing."

If only a man could see his God in such a light! How happy, how calm, how safe he would be! He would then truly have a God from whom he would know with certainty that all his fortunes—whatever they might be—had come to him and were still coming to him under the guidance of God's most gracious will. The word of Peter stands firm, "He cares for you." Can we hear a sweeter sound than this word? Therefore he says, "Cast all your cares upon him."

However, if we fail to do this and then presume to care for ourselves, what else are we then doing but seeking to obstruct God's care for us, and at the same time creating for ourselves a life of sorrow and labor, troubled with unrest and many fears and cares? And it is so futile! We accomplish nothing good thereby, as the Preacher says, "It is vanity of vanities, and vexation of the spirit" [Eccles. 1:2, 14]. Indeed, this entire book treats this experience, for it is written by one who himself tried out many things but found them all to be nothing but toil, vanity, and affliction of the spirit. He finally came to the conclusion that it is a gift of God when a man may eat and drink and live joyfully with his wife, that is, when he passes his days without anxiety and commits his care to God.[35]

Therefore, we ought to have no other care for ourselves except this, namely, that we do not care for ourselves or rob God of his care

---

[34] *Confessions*, viii, 11.
[35] Cf. Eccles. 5:18; 9:7, 9.

for us. Whatever remains to be said will easily be gathered from the corresponding image of evil (as I have said) and from recalling one's entire past life.

Chapter Four: The Fourth Image

The Infernal Blessing, or the Blessing Beneath Us

Thus far we have considered the blessings which are ours and which are within ourselves. Let us now look at the blessings that are found in others and which lie outside of us. The first is found in those who are beneath us, that is, in the dead and the damned. Isn't it strange that some kind of blessing can be found in them? However, the power of divine goodness is everywhere so great that it enables us to discern blessings even in the greatest evils.

First of all, as we compare the lot of the damned with our own, we see how immeasurable our gain is. This may be gathered readily from the corresponding image of evils. Great as the evils of death and hell are that we see in the damned, so great certainly are the gains that we see in ourselves, and the greater our blessings, the worse are their evils. These matters must not be glossed over with a light heart, for they forcibly commend to us the most wonderful mercy of God. If we deem them lightly, we run the danger of being found ungrateful, of being condemned together with these men, and of being even more cruelly tormented. Therefore, the more we perceive how they suffer and lament, the more we ought to rejoice in the goodness of God toward us, in keeping with Isaiah 65 [:13-15], "Behold, my servants shall eat, but you shall be hungry; behold, my servants shall drink, but you shall be thirsty; behold, my servants shall rejoice, but you shall be ashamed; behold, my servants shall sing for joy of heart, but you shall cry for sorrow of heart and shall wail for anguish of spirit. You shall leave your name as a curse to my chosen, etc." In short, as I have said, the examples of those who die in their sins and are damned are useful to us as an admonition and instruction (as St. Gregory[36] also observes in his *Dialogs*):

---

[36] Gregory I, known as "the Great" (*ca.* 540-604), reigned as pope from 590 to 604.

Happy are they who caution gain

From that which caused another's pain.[37]

Because it is so common and so well known, this blessing probably affects us but little. Nevertheless, it is numbered among the highest blessings and esteemed more than lightly by those who have an understanding heart. A great portion of all the Holy Scriptures deals with this, namely, the passages that speak of the wrath, the judgments, and the warnings of God. These wholesome teachings are confirmed for us most salutarily by the example of these wretched men. These examples are especially effective when we enter into the feelings of those who endure such things and put ourselves in the place of these people. Then they will move and admonish us to praise the goodness of God, who has preserved us from such evils.

Let us also compare them with God himself, so that we may see the divine justice in their case. Although this is a difficult task, it must be attempted. Now, since God is a just judge, we must love and laud his justice and rejoice in God even when he miserably destroys the wicked in body and soul, for in all this his lofty and unspeakable justice shines forth. Thus even hell is no less full of good, the supreme good, than is heaven. The justice of God is God himself and God is the highest good. Therefore, even as his mercy, so must his justice or judgment be loved, praised, and glorified above all things. In this sense David says, "The righteous will rejoice when he sees the vengeance, and he will wash his hands in the blood of the sinner" [Ps. 58:10]. For the same reason the Lord forbade Samuel in I Samuel 16 [:1] to continue mourning for Saul, saying, "How will you mourn over Saul when I have rejected him from reigning over Israel?" It is as if he says: Does my will so displease you that you prefer the will of man to me? In brief, this is the voice of praise and joy that resounds through the whole Psalter —namely, that the Lord is the judge of the widow and the father of the fatherless, that he will be the defense of the poor and the protector of the helpless, that the enemy shall be confounded and the ungodly destroyed, and many similar sayings.[38] If anyone, in

---

[37] *Books of Dialogs (Dialogorum libri),* IV.
[38] Cf. Ps. 10:14; 68:5; 140:12.

foolish pity, should feel compassion for that generation that kills the righteous, yes, even the Son of God, or for the crowd of wicked men, he will be found to be rejoicing in their iniquity and approving their actions. He deserves to perish in a manner like those whose sins he would condone. Let such a man hear the words from II Samuel 19 [:6], "You love those who hate you and hate those who love you." Joab spoke these words to David when he grieved too greatly over his ungodly and murderous son Absolom.

Therefore, in this image we ought to rejoice in the godliness of all the saints and in the justice of God, who very justly punishes the persecutors of their godliness and thereby delivers his elect out of their hands. Thus you see not small blessings, but the very greatest blessings shining forth from the dead and the damned, namely, the avenging of the injuries of all the saints, and yours as well, if, along with them, you are also righteous. What wonder, then, if by way of your present evil God punishes your enemy, that is, the sin in your body? You ought rather to rejoice in this work of God's supreme justice, which even without your prayer slays and destroys your fiercest foe, namely, the sin that is within you. But if you should feel pity for it, you will be found to be a friend of sin and an enemy of the justice at work in you. Guard against this strongly, lest it also be said of you that you love those who hate you and hate those who love you. Therefore, just as you ought to consent with joy to the justice of God raging against your own sin, so you should also approve of the justice which rages against the sinner, the enemy of all men and of God. Thus you see that the greatest blessings may be found in the greatest evils, and that we can rejoice in the greatest evils not because of the evils themselves, but because of the supreme goodness of God's justice which avenges us.

Chapter Five: The Fifth Image

The Blessing on Our Left Hand

Having discussed in the previous chapters those adversaries who are already damned and given over to the devils, we now come to discuss those who are still in this life. It is necessary to view them with other feelings and to find in them a twofold blessing.

The first is that they so abound in temporal goods that the prophets are almost moved to envy. Thus we read in Psalm 73 [:2-3], "But as for me, my feet almost stumbled, my steps had almost slipped, for I was envious of the unjust ones when I saw the peace which the sinners had." Later on he says, "Behold, these are the sinners who prosper in the world and increase in riches" [vs. 12]. Jeremiah says, "You are righteous, O Lord, when I dispute with you. However, I would discuss your judgments with you: 'Why does the way of the wicked prosper? Why are all who sin and act unjustly happy?'" [Jer. 12:1].

Why else does God lavish and waste so many blessings on them, except to comfort us thereby and to show how gracious he is to those "who are pure in heart," as is said in the same Psalm 73 [:1]? If he is that good to the wicked, how much more will he be good to those who are good! While he does not vex the wicked with any evil, he certainly does test the good with many evils so that they may acknowledge his goodness to them, not only in the blessings of the present, but even in those that are hidden and still to come, and so that they may say with the same psalmist, "It is good for me to draw near to God and to put my trust in the Lord" [Ps. 73:28]. It is as if he said: "Even though I endure a few sufferings from which I see those men to be free, I nevertheless trust that God is far more good to me than to them." Thus the visible blessings of the wicked are an incentive to us to hope for the blessings that are invisible and to disdain the evils that we suffer. In Matthew 6 [:26-30] Christ bids us to look at the birds of the air and the lilies of the field, saying, "If God, therefore, so clothes the grass which today is and tomorrow is cast into the oven, will he not much more clothe you, O men of little faith?" Hence, by comparing the blessings in which the wicked abound with the evils which we suffer, our faith is exercised and we receive God's consolation (which alone is holy): for the saints all things must work together for good [Rom. 8:28].

The other blessing, even more marvelous, is that in the providence of God the evils of our adversaries become blessings to us. Though their sins are a stumbling block to the weak, to the strong they are an exercise of their virtue, an opportunity for conflict, and the amassing of greater merit. "Blessed is the man who endures trials, for when he has stood the test he shall receive the crown of life" [Jas. 1:12]. What greater trial can there be than the host of evil examples? For this reason the world is called one of the enemies of God's saints, because with its enticements and ungodly works it incites, provokes, and lures us from the way of God to its own way. Thus we read in Genesis 6 [:2], "The sons of God saw that the daughters of men were fair," and they were made flesh. And in Numbers 25 [:1] we read, "The sons of Israel were at once with the daughters of the Moabites."

Thus it is good for us always to be oppressed with some trouble, lest in our weakness we succumb to the offenses of the world and fall into sin. Thus Lot is praised by Peter in II Peter 2 [:7-8] because in suffering much from the evil examples of the Sodomites, he thereby made progress in his righteousness. It is necessary for such offenses to come to furnish us with struggle and victory. But woe to the world because of its offenses [Matt. 18:7]. But if God procures such great blessings for us in the sins of others, ought we not in our hearts believe that he will work much greater blessings for us in our own troubles, even though our flesh and blood judge it to be otherwise!

The blessing which the world confers on us from another side of its evils is by no means smaller, namely, its adversities. When the world is unable to swallow us up with its allurements or make us one with itself through its offenses, it endeavors by means of suffering to drive us out and by means of pain to cast us off. It is always intent on ensnaring us by the example of its sins or by visiting its fury upon us through the torment of its pain. This is indeed the monster Chimera, whose head is maidenly and seductive, but whose body is that of a cruel lion and whose tail is that of a deadly serpent.[39] For the end of the world, both of its pleasures and its tyranny, is poison and eternal death.

Therefore, even as God enables us to find our blessings in the sins of the world, so also are its persecutions intended to increase

---

[39] Luther here merges the Homeric figures of the Chimera (*The Iliad*, 6, 179), a beast which had the head of a lion, the body of a goat, and the tail of a dragon, with that of the Sirens (*The Odyssey*, 12, 39).

our blessings, so that they may not be fruitless or in vain. Thus the very things that work us harm are turned to our profit. Concerning the innocents murdered by Herod [Matt. 2:16-18], St. Augustine says that Herod could never have done as much good with his favor as he did with his hatred.[40] St. Agatha went triumphantly to prison as if it were a banquet hall, pleading in this manner, "Unless you cause my body to be broken by your executioner, my soul will not be able to enter paradise bearing the Victor's palm, even as a grain of wheat, unless it is stripped of its husk and harshly beaten on the threshing floor, is not gathered into the barn." [41]

But why waste words here when we see that all of Scripture, the writings and statements of all the fathers, and the lives and deeds of all the saints agree on this matter, namely, that those who inflict the greatest harm on the believers are their greatest benefactors, as long as they bear their sufferings in the right spirit. That is why St. Peter says in I Peter 3 [:13], "And who is there who might harm you if you are followers of that which is good?" And in Psalm 89 [:22] we read, "The enemy shall accomplish nothing in him, nor shall the son of iniquity do harm to him." But how is it that he shall not harm us, seeing that he often even kills us? Simply because in harming us, he is working us the greatest gain. Thus, if we are wise, we find ourselves dwelling in the midst of blessings, and yet, at the same time, in the midst of evils. All things are so wondrously tempered under the providence of God's goodness!

The Sixth Chapter: The Sixth Image

The Blessings on Our Right Hand

This is the church of the saints, the new creation of God, our brothers and our friends, in whom we see nothing but blessing and nothing but consolation, though not always with the eyes of the flesh (thus they would appear in the corresponding image of evil), but

---

[40] Luther may have had in mind Augustine's *Harmony on the Gospels*, 6.
[41] The historical existence of Agatha, whose festival day (February 5) is observed chiefly in southern Italy and Sicily, is doubtful. On the statement attributed to her, see *BG* 6, 52, n. 2.

with the eyes of the spirit. Nevertheless, we must not disregard even these visible blessings of theirs, but rather learn that God wants to comfort us with them. Even Psalm 73 [:15] does not venture to condemn all those who acquire riches in this world when it says, "If I had said this, I would have rejected the generation of your children." That is, if I should consider wicked all those who possess wealth, health, and honor, I should be condemning even your saints, of whom there are so many. The Apostle instructs Timothy to admonish the rich of this world not to be haughty, but he does not forbid them to be rich [I Tim. 6:17]. The Scriptures remind us that Abraham, Isaac, and Jacob were rich men. Daniel and his companions held places of honor even in Babylon [Dan. 2:48-49]. Moreover, many kings of Judah were saintly men. It is with reference to them that the psalmist says, "If I had said this, I would have rejected the generation of your children."

I say that God gives an abundance of such blessings even to his people to comfort them and others. Still, these things are not their true blessings, but only shadows and signs of their real blessings, which are faith, hope, love, and other gifts and graces, which are shared with all through love.

This is the communion of saints in which we glory. Whose heart will not be lifted up, even in the midst of great evils, when he believes the very truth, namely, that the blessings of all the saints are his blessings, and his evil is also theirs? That is the very pleasant picture the Apostle paints in his word to the Galatians, "Bear one another's burdens and so fulfil the law of Christ" [Gal. 6:2]. Is it not a blessing for us to be in a company where "if one member (as is said in I Corinthians 12 [:26]) suffers, all members suffer together, and if one member is honored, all members rejoice together?" Therefore, when I suffer, I do not suffer alone, but Christ and all Christians suffer with me, for Christ says, "He who touches you, touches the apple of my eye" [Zech. 2:8]. Thus others bear my burden, and their strength is my strength. The faith of the church comes to the aid of my fearfulness; the chastity of others endures the temptation of my flesh; the fastings of others are my gain; the prayer of another pleads for me. In brief, such care do the members show one another that the more honorable members cover,

161

serve, and honor the less respected members, as is so beautifully set forth in I Corinthians 12 [:22-26].

Consequently, I can actually glory in the blessings of others as though they were my very own. They are truly mine when I am grateful and joyful with the others. It may be that I am base and ugly, while those whom I love and admire are fair and beautiful. By my love I make not only their blessings but their very selves my own. By their honor my shame is now made honorable, my want is supplied by their abundance, and my sins are healed by their merits.

Who could then despair in his sins? Who would not rejoice in his sorrows? He no longer bears his sin and punishment—and if he does bear them he does not bear them alone—but is supported by so many holy children of God, yes, by Christ himself. So great a thing is the communion of saints in the church of Christ.

If a person does not believe that this is a fact and that it happens, he is an infidel and has denied Christ and the church. Even if it is not perceived, it is still true. But who could fail to perceive it? After all, why do you not despair and become impatient? Is it due to your strength? By no means. It is because of the communion of saints. Otherwise, you could not even bear a venial sin,[42] or endure what men say against you. So close to you are Christ and the church! It is this that we confess in the Creed: "I believe in the Holy Spirit, the holy, catholic church." What else is it to believe in the holy church but to believe in the communion of saints? What is it that the saints have in common? Blessings, to be sure, and evils. All things belong to all, as symbolized in the bread and wine of the Sacrament of the Altar, where we are told by the Apostle that we are one body, one bread, one cup.[43] Who can hurt one part of the body without hurting the whole body? What pain can be suffered by the little toe that is not felt by the whole body. We are one body. Whatever another suffers, I also suffer and endure. Whatever

---

[42] According to Roman Catholic teaching, venial sin is "a less serious offense against the law of God." Such sin does not deprive the soul of sanctifying grace and can be pardoned without sacramental confession. Cf. *A Catechism of Christian Doctrine: Revised Edition of the Baltimore Catechism, No. 3* (1949), pp. 50-52.

[43] Cf. I Cor. 10:16-17.

good befalls him, befalls me. Thus Christ says that whatever is done unto one of the least of his brethren is done unto him [Matt. 25:40]. When a man receives only the smallest morsel of the bread in the sacrament, is he not said to partake of the bread? And if he despises one crumb of the bread, is he not said to have despised the bread?

Therefore, when we feel pain, when we suffer, when we die, let us turn to this, firmly believing and certain that it is not we alone, but Christ and the church who are in pain and are suffering and dying with us. Christ does not want us to be alone on the road of death, from which all men shrink. Indeed, we set out upon the road of suffering and death accompanied by the entire church. Actually, the church bears it more bravely than we do. Thus we can truthfully apply to ourselves the words Elisha spoke to his fearful servants, "Fear not, for those who are with us are more numerous than those with them. And Elisha prayed and said, 'Lord, open the eyes of the young man that he may see.' And the Lord opened his eyes and he saw. And behold, the mountain was full of horses and chariots of fire around Elisha" [II Kings 6:16-17].

All that remains for us now is to pray that our eyes, that is, the eyes of our faith, may be opened that we may see the church around us. Then there will be nothing for us to fear, as is also said in Psalm 125 [:2], "As mountains are round about it, so the Lord is round about his people, from this time forth and forever." Amen.

The Seventh Chapter: The Seventh Image

The Supernal Blessing, or the Blessing Above Us

I do not now speak of the eternal and heavenly blessings which the blessed enjoy in the perfect wisdom of God. If I speak of them at all I do so only in faith and insofar as they come within the realm of my understanding.

This seventh image is Jesus Christ, the King of glory, rising from the dead, just as in his suffering, death, and burial he formed the seventh image of evils. Here the heart can find its supreme joy and lasting possessions. Here there is not the slightest trace of evil, for "Christ being risen from the dead, will not die again. Death

163

no longer has dominion over him" [Rom. 6:9]. Here is that furnace of love and the fire of God in Zion, as Isaiah says, for Christ is not only born to us, but also given to us [Isa. 9:6]. Therefore, his resurrection and everything that he accomplished through it are mine. In Romans 8 [:32] the Apostle exults in exuberant joy, "Has he not also given me all things with him?"

What is it that he has wrought by his resurrection? He has destroyed sin and raised up righteousness, abolished death and restored life, conquered hell and bestowed everlasting glory on us. These blessings are so incalculable that the mind of man hardly dares believe that they have been granted to us. So it was with Jacob in Genesis 45 [:26–28]. When he heard that his son Joseph was ruler over Egypt, he was like a person awakened from deep slumber. Though they repeated all the words of Joseph, he did not believe them until they showed him the wagons that Joseph had sent. It would truly be just as difficult for us to believe that in Christ such great blessings have been bestowed upon us, if he had not taught us to believe it by many words and the testimony of our own experience, which are like the wagons of Joseph, and in the case of the disciples by his many appearances [I Cor. 15:1-8]. Christ is certainly the most precious "wagon," made by God for our righteousness, sanctification, redemption, and wisdom, as the Apostle declares in I Corinthians 1 [:30]. I am a sinner, but I am borne by his righteousness which is given to me. I am unclean, but his holiness is my sanctification, in which I ride gently. I am an ignorant fool, but his wisdom carries me forward. I deserve condemnation, but I am set free by his redemption, which is a safe wagon for me.

Thus the Christian (if he but believes it) may glory in the merits of Christ and in all his blessings as though he himself had won them. So truly are they his own that he can boldly dare to look forward to the judgment of God, however unbearable that is. Such a great thing is faith, such blessings does it bring us, such glorious sons of God does it make us! We cannot be sons without also inheriting our Father's blessings. Let Christians thus say in full confidence, "O death, where is your victory? O death, where is your sting?" namely, sin. "The sting of death is sin, and the strength of sin is the law. But thanks be to God who gave us the victory through

Jesus Christ, our Lord" [I Cor. 15:55-57]. That is to say, the law makes us sinners and sin makes us guilty of death. Who has conquered these two? Was it our righteousness? Was it our life? No, it was Jesus Christ, rising from death, condemning sin and death, imparting his righteousness to us, bestowing his merits on us, and holding his hand over us. Now all is well with us; we fulfil the law and vanquish sin and death. For all of this let there be honor, praise, and thanksgiving to God for ever and ever. Amen.

This, then, is the most sublime image, for in it we are lifted up not only above our evils, but even above our blessings, and we are set down in the midst of strange blessings gathered by the labors of another, whereas formerly we lay among evils that were also brought about by the sin of another and enlarged by our own [Rom. 5:17]. We are set down, I say, in Christ's righteousness, with which he himself is righteous, because we cling to that righteousness whereby he himself is acceptable to God, intercedes for us as our mediator, and gives himself wholly to us as our high priest and protector. Therefore, just as it is impossible for Christ with his righteousness not to please God, so it is impossible for us, with our faith clinging to his righteousness, not to please him. It is in this way that a Christian becomes almighty lord of all, having all things and doing all things, wholly without sin.[44] Even if he is in sins, these cannot do him harm; they are forgiven for the sake of the inexhaustible righteousness of Christ that removes all sins. It is on this that our faith relies, firmly trusting that he is such a Christ as we have described. He who does not believe this is like a deaf man hearing a story. He does not know Christ, neither does he understand what blessings are his nor how they may be enjoyed.

If we consider it properly and with an attentive heart, this one image—even if there were no other—suffices to fill us with such comfort that we should not only not grieve over our evils, but should also glory in our tribulations, scarcely feeling them for the joy that we have in Christ [Rom. 5:2-3]. May Jesus Christ, our Lord and God, blessed forevermore, instruct us in such glorying. Amen.

---

[44] On the Christian's lordship over all things (domini sumus), see The Freedom of a Christian (1520). LW 31, 327-377.

The End

With these trifles of mine, Most Illustrious Prince, and in token of my willingness to serve your Lordship to the best of my poor ability, I commend myself to Your Illustrious Lordship, ever ready to offer better service if my mental powers ever should equal my desires. I shall always remain a debtor to every neighbor of mine, but most of all to your Lordship, whom our Lord Jesus Christ in his merciful kindness may long preserve to us, and at last by a blessed death take home unto himself. Amen.

Your Most Illustrious Lordship's Intercessor,
BROTHER MARTIN LUTHER
Augustinian at Wittenberg

SERMON ON
THE WORTHY RECEPTION
OF THE SACRAMENT

1521

Translated by Martin H. Bertram

INTRODUCTION

By January, 1521, Martin Luther was a full-fledged heretic, condemned and excommunicated by the Roman pontiff[1] and under virtual condemnation by the emperor. Nonetheless, German rulers participating in the Imperial Diet at Worms succeeded in their effort to win a hearing and pass of safe conduct for Luther. Shortly after this maneuver, on March 10, 1521, it became quite clear that the monk from Wittenberg could not possibly be acquitted of the charges against him. Acting on his own initiative, Emperor Charles V issued an edict which ordered the confiscation and burning of Luther's writings.[2] On April 2 Luther left Wittenberg for Worms and his confrontation with the emperor and papal representatives.

Less than a week before his departure for Worms, on Maundy Thursday, March 28, Luther preached the sermon presented here. The fact that Luther was about to set out on a momentous and perilous journey is nowhere evident in the sermon's content. He sticks to his theme, and in serious pastoral fashion he speaks out against the prevalent lay abuse of the Lord's Supper. This abuse was rooted, according to Luther, in the reception of the sacrament out of obedience to the command of the church and out of the desire to achieve certain personal ends. The sacrament, Luther says, is not and should not be for those who come solely because they are commanded to do so, but for those who recognize their personal need and are inwardly driven to receive it. Recognition of his sinfulness and unworthiness should not prevent a man's reception of the sacrament. Indeed, the Lord Jesus Christ intended his Supper precisely for sinners who trust and believe in the words of institution. Thus Luther

---

[1] The papal bull *Exsurge, Domine* was signed on June 15, 1520. A sixty day period of grace was extended to Luther, beginning with the public nailing of the bull to the doors of the Church of St. John Lateran and the apostolic chancery in Rome, and the cathedrals of Brandenburg, Meissen, and Merseburg. Luther publicly burned the document on December 10, 1520. On the difficulty of publishing the bull in Germany, see E. G. Schwiebert, *Luther and His Times* (St. Louis: Concordia Publishing House, 1950), pp. 484-485.

[2] Cf. A. Kluckhohn and A. Wrede, *Deutsche Reichstagsakten unter Karl V* (4 vols.; Gotha, 1896), II, 529.

the pastor invites Christians to come to the Lord's Supper, not in fear or for reward, but with faith and trust in Christ's desire and power to heal them.

Poliander's[3] collection of Luther's sermons contains a version of this discourse,[4] which, while at times quoting the text followed here, is generally more detailed and polemical. It should be noted, however, that Poliander gives only three points, whereas our text contains thirteen.

The translation is based on the German text, *Sermon von der würdigen Empfahung des heiligen wahren Leichnams Christi, gethan am Gründonnerstag*, in WA 7, (689) 692-697.

---

[3] John Poliander (or Gramann, 1486-1541), who was secretary to John Eck, Luther's opponent at the Leipzig Debate, was so impressed by Luther that he gave up his position at the St. Thomas School in Leipzig to study theology at Wittenberg. While at Wittenberg he and fellow students noted down and compiled many of Luther's sermons.

[4] For the Poliander version, see WA 9, 640-647.

SERMON ON
THE WORTHY RECEPTION
OF THE SACRAMENT

Jesus

First, those who openly live in sin or who wilfully harbor evil thoughts, such as of hatred, of uncleanness, and the like, shall not receive the sacrament. Until they shun these sins, the church's precept is not meant for them. It is better to obey God's command than that of the church [Acts 5:29]. It is better to refrain from receiving the sacrament than to receive it and thereby sin against God's commandment, which forbids the holy sacrament to such sinners.[1]

Second, those who find that they are prompted to partake of it merely because of the order of the church[2] or from habit, who, if wholly free to choose, would not come to it with good will and longing, also must not partake of the sacrament. As St. Augustine says, the sacrament seeks a hungry, thirsty, and desirous soul which yearns for it.[3] But those who go only because of command or out of habit feel no desire or longing for it, but rather horror or dread, so that they would rather be away from it than near it. A person with a yearning heart does not wait for a command, nor is he moved by precept or habit. Such a man is driven by his need and his desire. He has his mind fixed only on the sacrament, which he desires.

Third, you may say that if this is true, then there is reason to fear that only a few people in the world receive the sacrament

---

[1] The "commandment" Luther had in mind may be I Cor. 11:28-29.
[2] Cf. *The Misuse of the Mass* (1521). LW 36, 127-230. Cf. also LW 51, 93; LW 53, 31. On the frequency of sacramental celebrations and practices related to Holy Communion during the Middle Ages, see Helmut T. Lehmann (ed.), *Meaning and Practice of the Lord's Supper* (Philadelphia: Fortress Press, 1961), pp. 75-112.
[3] *Preaching on Psalm 21 (Enarratio in psalmos xxi).*

worthily, since almost everybody receives it not by free choice but only in obedience to the church. Answer: that does not alter facts. There must be hunger and thirst for this food and drink; otherwise harm is sure to follow. The same is true in nature. When your body is sated and filled, and yet you partake of a plentiful and rich meal, this is bound to end in sickness and death. But if your body is hungry and thirsty, such a meal will make you cheerful, healthy, and strong.

Fourth, the pope falls short of his duty, yes, he does wrong, by indiscriminately driving and ordering the people to the sacrament rather than first doing all in his power to instil this hunger and thirst in their hearts. Thus he simply ruins souls and drives them to sin, utterly defeating the purpose of the sacrament unless we understand the pope's command as applying only to those who hunger for the sacrament. If that is not the meaning, it is indeed an evil and harmful command; it should be ignored until your own hunger constrains you to come to the sacrament. Then you will no longer need the pope's command. After all, the sacrament—even God himself—can bestow nothing on you against your will. Since God's gifts are so great, they demand a great hunger and desire, but they avoid and flee from a forced and unwilling heart.

Fifth, such hunger and thirst are created not by compelling a man, but by showing him his frailty and his need so that he will see his wretched condition and feel the desire to be delivered from it. This happens, for instance, when you recognize that you are weak in faith, cold in love, and faint in hope. You will find that you are disposed toward hatred and impatience, impurity, greed, and whatever other vice there is. This you will undoubtedly find and feel if you really look at yourself. All the saints have found this to be true about themselves. You must also see whether you have weakly yielded or would have fallen prey to one or the other. To know and understand your sin and to be willing to resolve to get rid of such vice and evil and to long to become pure, modest, gentle, mild, humble, believing, loving, etc.—that is the beginning of such hunger and thirst.[4]

---

[4] In a sermon on the Lord's Supper preached in 1528 Luther said, "Neither preacher, prince, pope, nor emperor compels me, but my great need and, beyond this, the benefit." *LW* 51, 192-193.

Sixth, the greater and more fervent this desire is in you, the better fit you are to receive the sacrament. God has given his commandment so that you might thereby know your sin. Moreover, he punishes some dreadfully and threatens others with death and hell and pain and misery to spur man on to long for godliness and thus prepare him for this sacrament. Then a man no longer heeds the church's command but is happy that he can partake of the sacrament because of his own urging and need, without any command or demand. The pope and all the priests should implant this doctrine and teaching in the people and leave their own precept aside, thus giving everybody a free hand. Then he who for such reasons does not long for the sacrament will not partake of it. Now, however, they stress only their command, and the people throng to it, and great harm is done to Christendom.

Seventh, when a man has this hunger and so is prepared for the sacrament, he must carefully avoid receiving it while trusting in his own worthiness. Nor must he merely pray, as some do, "Lord, I am not worthy to have you come under my roof; but say only a word, and my soul will be healed" [Matt. 8:8]. I am not rejecting that prayer, but one should be aware of something else. I am referring to the words Christ spoke when he instituted the mass: "Take, eat, this is my body which is given for you. Take, drink, all of you; for it is the cup of the new and eternal testament in my blood, poured out for you and for all for the forgiveness of sins" [Matt. 26:26-28].

Although the priest utters these words softly during mass[5] (would to God that he would shout them loudly so that all could hear them clearly, and, moreover, in the German language), every Christian should have these words close to himself and put his mind on them above all others. For just as they are meant for us all, so they are spoken by the priest in the stead of Christ to all who stand around him. We should take all of these words to heart, placing our trust in them and not doubting that with these the Lord invites us to be his guests at this abundant meal.

Eighth, the priest's elevation of the sacrament and the cup,

---

[5] This part of the mass was spoken inaudibly or "secretly."

together with the ringing of the bells,[6] has no other purpose than to remind us of the words of Christ. It is as if the priest and the bell-ringer were saying to us all, "Listen, you Christians, and see, take and eat, take and drink, etc. 'This is the body and this is the blood of Christ,' spoken softly by the priest, but heard clearly and audibly by us. With these words you must now edify your hungry heart and rely upon the truth of this divine promise, then receive the sacrament, make your way to God, and say, 'Lord, it is true that I am not worthy for you to come under my roof, but I need and desire your help and grace to make me godly. I now come to you, trusting only in the wonderful words I just heard, with which you invite me to your table and promise me, the unworthy one, forgiveness of all my sins through your body and blood if I eat and drink them in this sacrament. Amen. Dear Lord, I do not doubt the truth of your words. Trusting them, I eat and I drink with you. Do unto me according to your words. Amen.'"

Ninth, worthy reception of the sacrament, however, is not based on our diligence and effort, our work and prayers, or our fasting, but on the truth of the divine words. To be sure, some invented various fruits of the mass to stimulate a desire and longing for the sacrament. One devised this fruit, another that. Some among them write that he who comes to the mass will not grow older. They have fooled with it so long that they have made the fruits of the mass appear to be nothing but bodily and temporal benefits,[7] although they have no authority beyond their own dreams to do this. They also believe that the mass assures security and happiness for the day on which it is heard. Nothing has remained of the mass, that is, of the meaning and use of this divine promise, which is really the whole essence of the mass. For during the Last Supper the Lord instituted only these words, and he gave them to us solely for spiritual purposes, such as, the remission of sin and the reception

---

[6] On the elevation of the host, which marked the moment of transsubstantiation, see LW 54, 461-462. The practice of elevation was abolished at Wittenberg in 1542.

[7] In A Treatise on the New Testament, That Is, the Holy Mass (1520), Luther enumerates other temporal benefits generally attributed to the sacrament in the popular mind and adds that the sacrament has degenerated into a kind of "witchcraft." Cf. LW 35, 75-111, especially p. 92, n. 17.

of grace and help so that the human heart, clinging to these words by faith, should gain strength in everything good against sin, death, and hell. His Word and work were not intended to help us in a temporal way, but in a spiritual and eternal way. It is an insult to God to misuse these for the attainment of temporal benefits.

Tenth, when the pastor administers the sacrament, it must be understood that he is acting in accord with Christ's words, "Take, and eat," etc. A person should receive the sacrament on the strength of these words, be mindful of them, and not doubt that in him there takes place the intent and content of those same words of Christ, namely, that Christ's body is given for him and that his blood was shed for him, and that he is an heir of the New Testament, that is, of God's grace and favor for eternal life. Faith creates godliness and drives out all sin, grants strength in sickness, enlightens in all blindness, heals all evil inclinations, guards against sin, and performs every good deed. In brief, the fruit of such faith is that never can there remain any frailty; for in faith the Holy Spirit is given, and thereby a man loves God because of the abundant goodness received from him. A man becomes cheerful and glad to do all that is good without the compulsion of law and command.

Eleventh, just see how far those who taught us that if we wanted to receive the sacrament worthily we would have to be perfectly pure[8] have departed from the proper path. They made us shy and timid. They reduced the sweet and blessed sacrament to a frightful and hazardous act. As a result, only a few people come to the sacrament with joy and longing, since they constantly fear that they are not pure and worthy enough.[9] It is just this worry and fear that makes them unworthy and, at the same time, drives out hunger and thirst. Fear and desire cannot exist side by side. Thus they hindered us with the very means by which they thought to advance us. If you do not want to come to the sacrament until

---

[8] For example, absolution following a valid confession is a Roman Catholic prerequisite for the right reception of the sacrament. Cf. *A Catechism of Christian Doctrine: Revised Edition of the Baltimore Catechism, No. 3.*

[9] Cf. Luther's sermon of 1528 on the Lord's Supper: "Don't say: I am not fit today, I will wait a while. This is a trick of the devil. What will you do if you are not fit when death comes? Who will make you fit then?" *LW* 51, 192. See also this volume, p. 102.

you are perfectly clean and whole, it would be better for you to remain away entirely. The sacrament is to purify you and help you. Yet you do not want to come until you no longer need its help and have already helped yourself. This is just as if you were invited to a splendid banquet and would gorge and swill before you went. Then, as you sit at table, you would feel nauseated and miserable, while all the fine dishes would be served you in vain. How would your host like that?

Twelfth, you see, that is what happens when one tries to make people pious and lead them to the right by means of commandments and laws. It only makes them worse. Thanks to such tactics, they do unwillingly and drearily whatever they do. This becomes a hindrance to God's grace and sacrament. God neither wants to nor will he grant this grace to those who were forced, pressed, and driven to the sacrament by commandment and law, but only to hearts that long and pine and thirst for it, to hearts that come voluntarily. In Matthew 11 [:12] Christ says, "Since the days of John the Baptist the kingdom of heaven has suffered violence, and men of violence took it by force." That is to say: Since John showed the people their sins and shortcomings, which all pastors should do, they longed so for the kingdom of God and its help that they immediately and forcefully pressed toward it and seized it. God loves such guests; they who are thus hounded by their sins and transgressions are welcome to him. Psalm 39 [42:1] reads, "As a hunted hart longs for a fountain of fresh water, so my soul longs for thee, O God."

Thirteenth, Christ entices us similarly in Matthew 11 [:28], saying, "Come to me, all you who labor and are heavy-laden, and I will refresh and help you." It is out of the question that the Lord is here speaking about physical labor or burdens, for he helps only the soul. Therefore, these words of his must be understood to refer to the labor and the burden of the conscience, which is nothing else than a bad conscience oppressed by sins committed, by daily transgressions, and by a leaning toward sin. The Lord does not drive all such people from him, as do those who teach that we must come to the sacrament with purity and worthiness. Nor does he issue a command or compel anyone to go to the sacrament, but rather he

176

kindly invites and encourages all who are sinners and find themselves burdened and who yearn for help. The sublime sacrament must be regarded by us not as a poison, but as a medicine for the soul.[10] Christ himself declares in Matthew 9 [:12], "Those who are well have no need of a physician, but those who are sick." The only question is whether you thoroughly recognize and feel your labor and your burden and that you yourself fervently desire to be relieved of these. Then you are indeed worthy of the sacrament. If you believe, the sacrament gives you everything you need. At present, however, most people come to the sacrament without this understanding of it. They come with a hungry stomach and a full soul; they pray much beforehand and yet do not believe. They receive the sacrament and yet do not really avail themselves of it. They have no other reason for receiving the sacrament than a fearful and unwilling obedience to the church's precept, thus becoming utterly unfit for it. Woe unto all teachers who not only are silent about the use and power of the holy sacrament, but also are a hindrance to it with their mad doings and writings. May God deliver us from them. Amen.

Finis

---

[10] Cf. *LW* 51, 192.

COMFORT WHEN FACING
GRAVE TEMPTATIONS

1521

Translated by Martin H. Bertram

INTRODUCTION

In this brief treatise Luther deals with a subject which was quite familiar to him: spiritual assault and distress. Luther uses the word *Anfechtung,* which has no exact English equivalent and is more inclusive and radical than the word "temptation." More than enticement or inducement, *Anfechtung* is an assault on either the body, mind, or soul, involving fear, conscience, sin, or guilt, and is always a test of one's faith. *Anfechtung* can stem from the devil,[1] or from the "hidden God," who "has a way at times of playing and toying in a friendly manner with his own . . . to test us."[2] Roland Bainton defines it as "all the doubts, turmoil, pang, tremor, pains, despair, desolation, and desperation which invade the spirit of man." [3]

Luther does not define or analyze the particular nature of the assault and distress this piece deals with. He seems to assume that his readers know exactly what he means, and he launches immediately into the subject at hand.

There is considerable uncertainty about the date of this treatise. The oldest extant printed copy is in a book of one hundred twenty-eight pages, published in 1545, containing "Several Writings and Sermons of Comfort for Those in Need, Near Death, and Facing Temptation." [4] The editor of this book was Caspar Cruciger.[5] No date was attached to the treatise; it was simply appended to a treatise from the year 1532. The treatise, however, was also included in a handwritten collection of Luther's sermons, written down by an unknown person but edited by Poliander.[6] Here the date 1521 is given. There seems to be no substantial reason for rejecting this date, and so the year of the great confrontation at the Diet of

---

[1] *LW* 51, 179-180.
[2] *WA* 53, 475-476.
[3] *Here I Stand* (Nashville: Abingdon Press, 1952), p. 42. See also *LW* 48, 28, n. 10.
[4] See *LW* 7, 779.
[5] Caspar Cruciger (1504-1548) was a member of the group which worked with Luther in translating Scripture. He was also one of the editors of the Wittenberg Edition of Luther's Works.
[6] See p. 170, n. 3.

Worms is accepted as the year in which Luther wrote this pastoral piece. Luther himself probably wrote none of the extant versions; they were copied down by his associates either from his oral delivery or from an original manuscript.

By the same token, it is not clear what circumstances motivated this particular writing. The message of the treatise, however, is quite clear. The comfort extended by Luther is rooted in the fact that the person assailed by temptation is a member of the communion of saints and is armed with God's Word. The tempted person, however, should realize that there is always a benefit that accrues to him from such assaults, although he dare not attempt to divine it. Finally, he invites the tempted person to a fuller faith in Christ, but Luther warns that before the trials subside, they will first flare to greater intensity.

The translation is based on the Cruciger German text, *Tröstung für eine Person in hohen Anfechtungen,* in WA 7, (779) 784-791, where the Poliander text is produced alongside the Cruciger text.

COMFORT WHEN FACING
GRAVE TEMPTATIONS

First, such a person[1] must by no means rely on himself, nor must he be guided by his own feelings. Rather, he must lay hold of the words offered to him in God's name, cling to them, place his trust in them, and direct all the thoughts and feelings of his heart to them.

Second, he must not imagine that he is the only one assailed about his salvation, but he must be aware (as St. Peter declares) that there are many more people in the world passing through the same trials [I Pet. 5:9]. How often does David lament and cry out in the Psalms, "O God, I am driven far from thy sight" [31:22], and, "I became like those who go into hell" [28:1]. These trials are not rare among the godly. They hurt, to be sure, but that is also in order, etc.

Third, he should by no means insist on deliverance from these trials without yielding to the divine will. He should address God cheerfully and firmly and say, "If I am to drink this cup, dear Father, may your will, not mine, be done" [Luke 22:42].

Fourth, there is no stronger medicine[2] for this than to begin with words such as David used when he said in Psalm 18 [:3], "I will call upon the Lord and praise him, and so shall I be saved from all that assails me." For the evil spirit of gloom cannot be driven away by sadness and lamentation and anxiety, but by praising God, which makes the heart glad.

Fifth, he must thank God diligently for deeming him worthy of such a visitation, of which many thousands of people remain deprived.[3] It would be neither good nor useful for man to know

---

[1] The Poliander text has the word "sister," suggesting that the treatise may have been written to someone but intended for a third person, a woman.

[2] The full title in the Poliander text is *A Comforting Medicine for People Faced with Grave Temptations, Temptations that Come from the Evil Foe.*

[3] Luther says elsewhere that the most dangerous trial is when there is none. *Treatise on Good Works* (1520). *LW* 44, 47 and 63.

183

what great blessings lie hidden under such trials. Some have wanted to fathom this and have thereby done themselves much harm. Therefore, we should willingly endure the hand of God in this and in all suffering. Do not be worried; indeed, such a trial is the very best sign of God's grace and love for man.[4] At such a time it is well to pray, read, or sing Psalm 142, which is especially helpful at this point.[5]

Psalm 142

I cry to the Lord with my voice,
with my voice I make supplication to the Lord.
I pour out my complaint before him,
 I lay my trouble before him,
When my spirit is filled with fear,
 thou comest to my aid.

(That is, thou hast concern about what happens to me and what should happen to me).

In the path where I walk
 they have placed a snare for me.
(The devil does that by means of evil thoughts which fill man with uncertainty as to his fate and hinder him in his being and doing. However, we must commit this to God, who knows well what our course will be.)

I look to the right and watch,
 there is no one who wants to know me.
(That is, the soul imagines that it does not belong in the company of the blessed.[6] Here where the blessed are, no one knows the soul. Now it would flee in an attempt to rid itself of this grief, but, as seen in the following, this is impossible.)

---

[4] Cf. Ps. 94:12; Heb. 12:6; and Rev. 3:19.
[5] The translation and exposition which follows is the only such work done by Luther on this psalm. See his suggestions concerning the translation of this psalm in WA, DB 3, 162, and his lecture notes on this psalm in WA 4, 441-442.
[6] The Poliander text has only "in their company." WA 7, 786.

I cannot escape.

(That is, there can be neither escape nor flight, and I must remain here in my fear.)

And no man is concerned about my soul.

(That is what the soul thinks, and that is also what it feels; but for all of that, the soul must not yield and give way to such thoughts and feelings.)

I cry to thee, dear Lord

(since nothing else wants to comfort or is able to help)

and I say, "Thou art my refuge,
my portion in the land of the living.

(That is, everything tells me that I must die and perish. But I fight against that and say, "No, I want to live, for this I look to thee in faith.")

Give heed to my lament,
for I am being greatly tormented.
Save me from my persecutors,
for they are too powerful for me.[7]
Lead my soul out of prison

(That is, out of the distress and terror which hold me captive.)

that I may give thanks to thy name.
The righteous will gather around me

(to offer thanks with me and for me as a lost sheep [Luke 15:6])

For thou dealest bountifully with me.

(That is, rendereth me comfort in my need and help against evil.)
Amen.

---

[7] The Poliander text adds, "That is, not only do people assail me, but the devil also is a clever accuser and deft jurist against my sins, and I, poor fellow that I am, cannot quote Scripture sufficiently against him. He wants to turn your mercy into nothing and my sins into mountains." WA 7, 788.

Sixth, it is necessary that one never doubt the promise of the truthful and faithful God. He promised to hear us, yes, he commanded us to pray, for the very reason that we might know and firmly believe that our petition will be heard. Thus Christ says in Matthew 21 [:22] and in Mark 11 [:24], "Therefore I tell you, whatever you ask in prayer, believe that you shall receive it, and you surely will." Also in Luke 11 [:9-13], "Ask, and it will be given you; seek, and you will find; knock, and it will be opened to you. What son is there among you, who would ask his father for bread, and he would offer him a stone instead? etc. If you then, who are evil, know how to give good gifts to your children, how much more will the heavenly Father give the Holy Spirit to those who ask him?"

Such a person must also know Christ aright and know that only by him alone are all our sins paid and God's grace given to us, lest he presume to deal directly with God and without this mediator.[8]

But if the inner assaults should become more severe after this medicine, he should do nothing else but abide by the above advice. For this grave temptation is a good omen that this will soon end and that the devil is very nearly vanquished. He is merely making his strongest attempt now. Pharaoh, too, never persecuted the children of Israel as severely as he did toward the end.[9] One can also see this in a physical illness. Just before the medicine begins to help and heal the person, it makes him extremely sick. Therefore this person should be hopeful and of good cheer.

---

[8] The Poliander text ends here.
[9] Cf. Exod. 1:8-14.

INDEXES

INDEX OF NAMES AND SUBJECTS

INDEX TO SCRIPTURE PASSAGES